P9-EKI-946

Digital Photography FOR DUMMIES®

SPECIAL EDITION

Based on Digital Photography For Dummies, 4th Edition

by Julie Adair King

WILEY

John Wiley & Sons Canada, Ltd

Digital Photography For Dummies, Special Edition

Published by
John Wiley & Sons Canada, Ltd
22 Worcester Road
Etobicoke, ON M9W 1L1
www.wiley.ca

Copyright © 2003 John Wiley & Sons Canada, Ltd. All rights reserved. No part of this book, including interior design, cover design, and icons, may be reproduced or transmitted in any form, by any means (electronic, photocopying, recording, or otherwise) without the prior written permission of the publisher.

National Library of Canada Cataloguing in Publication

King, Julie Adair

Digital photography for dummies / Julie Adair King. Special Edition.

Includes index.
ISBN 0-470-83357-2

1. Photography—Digital techniques. 2. Image processing—Digital techniques. 3. Digital cameras. I. Title.

TR267.K56 2003   778.3   C2003-901502-5

Printed in Canada

2 3 4 5 TRI 07 06 05 04 03

Distributed in Canada by John Wiley & Sons Canada, Ltd.

For general information on John Wiley & Sons Canada, Ltd., including all books published by Wiley Publishing, Inc., please call our warehouse, Tel 1-800-567-4797. For reseller information, including discounts and premium sales, please call our sales department, Tel 416-646-7992. For press review copies, author interviews, or other publicity information, please contact our marketing department, Tel: 416-646-4584, Fax 416-236-4448.

For authorization to photocopy items for corporate, personal, or educational use, please contact Cancopy, The Canadian Copyright Licensing Agency, One Yonge Street, Suite 1900, Toronto, ON, M5E 1E5 Tel 416-868-1620 Fax 416-868-1621; www.cancopy.com.

LIMIT OF LIABILITY/DISCLAIMER OF WARRANTY: WHILE THE PUBLISHER AND AUTHOR HAVE USED THEIR BEST EFFORTS IN PREPARING THIS BOOK, THEY MAKE NO REPRESENTATIONS OR WARRANTIES WITH RESPECT TO THE ACCURACY OR COMPLETENESS OF THE CONTENTS OF THIS BOOK AND SPECIFICALLY DISCLAIM ANY IMPLIED WARRANTIES OF MERCHANTABILITY OR FITNESS FOR A PARTICULAR PURPOSE. NO WARRANTY MAY BE CREATED OR EXTENDED BY SALES REPRESENTATIVES OR WRITTEN SALES MATERIALS. THE ADVICE AND STRATEGIES CONTAINED HEREIN MAY NOT BE SUITABLE FOR YOUR SITUATION. NEITHER THE PUBLISHER NOR AUTHOR SHALL BE LIABLE FOR ANY LOSS OF PROFIT OR ANY OTHER COMMERCIAL DAMAGES, INCLUDING BUT NOT LIMITED TO SPECIAL, INCIDENTAL, CONSEQUENTIAL, OR OTHER DAMAGES.

Trademarks: Wiley, the Wiley publishing logo. For Dummies, the Dummies Man logo, A Reference for the Rest of Us!, The Dummies Way, Dummies Daily, The Fun and Easy Way, Dummies.com and related trade dress are trademarks or registered trademarks of Wiley Publishing, Inc., in the United States, Canada and other countries, and may not be used without written permission. All other trademarks are the property of their respective owners. John Wiley & Sons Canada, Ltd is not associated with any product or vendor mentioned in this book.

Contents at a Glance

Publisher's Acknowledgments

We're proud of this book; please send us your comments at canadapt@wiley.com. Some of the people who helped bring this book to market include the following:

Acquisitions and Editorial

Executive Editor: Joan Whitman

Editor: Melanie Rutledge

Substantive and Copy Editor: Michael Kelly

New Business Development Manager: Christiane Coté

Production

Publishing Services Director: Karen Bryan

Project Manager: Elizabeth McCurdy

Project Coordinator: Abigail Brown

Layout and Graphics: Kim Monteforte, Heidy Lawrance Associates

Proofreader: Michael Kelly

Indexer: Belle Wong

John Wiley & Sons Canada, Ltd.

Bill Zerter, Chief Operating Officer

Robert Harris, Publisher, Professional and Trade Division

Publishing and Editorial for Consumer Dummies

Diane Graves Steele, Vice President and Publisher, Consumer Dummies

Joyce Pepple, Acquisitions Director, Consumer Dummies

Kristin A. Cocks, Product Development Director, Consumer Dummies

Michael Spring, Vice President and Publisher, Travel

Suzanne Jannetta, Editorial Director, Travel

Publishing for Technology Dummies

Andy Cummings, Acquisitions Director

Composition Services

Gerry Fahey, Executive Director of Production Services

Debbie Stailey, Director of Composition Services

Introduction

● ●

*T*he era of the digital camera has arrived, and with it comes a new and exciting way of thinking about photography. With a digital camera, a computer, and some photo-editing software, you can explore unlimited creative opportunities. You can easily bend and shape the image that comes out of your camera to suit your personal artistic vision. You can combine several pictures into a photographic collage, for example, and create special effects that are either impossible or difficult to achieve with film. You also can do your own photo retouching, handling tasks that once required a professional studio, such as cropping away excess background or sharpening focus.

More important, digital cameras make taking great pictures easier. Because most cameras have a monitor on which you can instantly review your shots, you can see right away whether you have a keeper or need to try again. No more picking up a packet of prints at the photo lab and discovering that you didn't get a single good picture of that first birthday party, or that incredible ocean sunset, or whatever it was that you wanted to capture.

Digital photography also enables you to share visual information with people around the world instantaneously. Literally minutes after snapping a digital picture, you can put the photo in the hands of friends, colleagues, or strangers across the globe by attaching it to an e-mail message or posting it on the World Wide Web.

Blending the art of photography with the science of the computer age, digital cameras serve as both an outlet for creative expression and a serious communication tool. Just as important, digital cameras are *fun*. And this book helps you capitalize on that fun, explaining what you need to know to become a successful digital photographer; from shooting and editing to publishing your pictures on the Web. And you don't need to be a computer or photography geek to understand what's going on. *Digital Photography For Dummies* speaks your language — plain English, that is — with a dash of humour thrown in to make things more enjoyable.

What's in This Book?

This book provides information that will help you select the right digital photography equipment and photo software. You can find chapters that help you use your camera to its best advantage. In addition, this book shows you how to perform certain photo-editing tasks, such as adjusting image brightness and contrast and creating photographic collages.

For some photo-editing techniques, the basic editing tools that I discuss function similarly from program to program, and the general approach to editing is the same no matter what program you use. So you can refer to this book for the solid foundation you need to understand different editing functions and then easily adapt the specific steps to your own photo software.

Although this book is designed for beginning- and intermediate-level digital photographers, I do assume that you have a little bit of computer knowledge. For example, you should understand how to start programs, open and close files, and get around in the Windows or Macintosh environment, depending on which type of operating system you use. If you're brand-new to computers as well as to digital photography, you may want to get a copy of the appropriate *For Dummies* title for your operating system, as an additional reference.

Here's a brief summary of the kind of information you can find in *Digital Photography For Dummies*.

Part I: Peering through the Digital Viewfinder

This part of the book gets you started on your digital photography adventure. The first two chapters describe what digital cameras can and can't do and how they perform their photographic magic. Chapter 3 introduces you to some of the camera add-ons and other accessories that make digital photography better, easier, or just more fun.

Part II: Ready, Set, Shoot!

Are you photographically challenged? Are your pictures too dark, too light, too blurry, or just plain boring? Before you fling your camera across the room in frustration, check out this part of the book.

Chapter 4 reveals the secret to capturing perfectly exposed, perfectly focused photographs and also presents tips to help you compose more powerful, more exciting images. Chapter 5 explores technical questions that arise on a digital photography shoot, such as what resolution and compression settings to choose. In addition, you find out how to take pictures that you plan to incorporate into a photo collage, capture a series of photographs that you can stitch together into a panorama, and handle problems such as shooting in fluorescent lighting and taking action shots.

Part III: From Camera to Computer and Beyond

After you fill up your camera with photos, you need to get them off the camera and out into the world. Chapters in this part of the book show you how to do just that.

Chapter 6 explains the process of transferring pictures to your computer and also discusses ways to store and catalogue all those images. Chapter 7 looks at ways to display and distribute images electronically — placing them on Web pages and attaching them to e-mail messages, for example.

Part IV: Tricks of the Digital Trade

In this part of the book, you get an introduction to photo editing. Chapter 8 discusses simple fixes for problem pictures. Of course, after reading the shooting tips in Chapters 4 and 5, you shouldn't wind up with many bad photos. But for the occasional stinker, Chapter 8 comes to the rescue by showing you how to adjust exposure and contrast, sharpen focus, and crop away unwanted portions of the image.

Chapter 9 presents some more-advanced tricks, including painting on your image, building photo collages, and applying special effects.

Part V: The Part of Tens

Information in this part of the book is presented in easily digestible, bite-sized nuggets. Chapter 10 contains the top ten ways to improve your digital photographs; Chapter 11 offers ten ideas for using digital images. In other words, Part V is perfect for the reader who wants a quick, yet filling, mental snack.

Icons Used in This Book

Like other books in the *For Dummies* series, this book uses icons to flag especially important information. Here's a quick guide to the icons used in *Digital Photography For Dummies*.

This icon marks stuff that you should commit to memory. Doing so will make your life easier and less stressful.

Text marked with this icon breaks technical gobbledygook down into plain English. In many cases, you really don't need to know this stuff, but boy, will you sound impressive if you do.

The Tip icon points you to shortcuts that help you avoid doing more work than necessary. This icon also highlights ideas for creating better pictures and working around common digital photography problems.

When you see this icon, pay attention — danger is on the horizon. Read the text next to a Warning icon to keep yourself out of trouble and to find out how to fix things if you leaped before you looked.

Conventions Used in This Book

In addition to icons, *Digital Photography For Dummies* follows a few other conventions. When I want you to choose a command from a menu, you see the menu name, an arrow, and then the command name. For example, if I want you to choose the Cut command from the Edit menu, I write it this way: "Choose Edit⇨Cut."

Sometimes, you can choose a command more quickly by pressing two or more keys on your keyboard than by clicking your way through menus. I present these keyboard shortcuts like so: "Press Ctrl+A," which simply means to press and hold down the Ctrl key, press the A key, and then let up on both keys. Usually, I provide the PC shortcut first, followed by the Mac shortcut, if it's different.

What Do I Read First?

The answer depends on you. You can start with Chapter 1 and read straight through to the Index, if you like. Or you can flip to whatever section of the book interests you most and start there.

Digital Photography For Dummies is designed so that you can grasp the content in any chapter without having to read all chapters that came before. So if you need information on a particular topic, you can get in and out as quickly as possible.

Part I

Peering through the Digital Viewfinder

In this part...

When I was in high school, the science teachers insisted that the only way to learn about different creatures was to cut them open and poke about their innards. In my opinion, dissecting dead things never accomplished anything other than giving the boys a chance to gross out the girls by pretending to swallow formaldehyde-laced body parts.

But even though I'm firmly against dissecting our fellow earthly beings, I am wholly in favour of dissecting new technology. It's my experience that if you want to make a machine work for you, you have to know what makes that machine tick. Only then can you fully exploit its capabilities.

To that end, this part of the book dissects the machine known as the digital camera. Chapter 1 looks at some of the pros and cons of digital photography, while Chapter 2 pries open the lid of a digital camera so that you can get a better understanding of how the thing performs its magic. Chapter 3 provides the same kind of close inspection of camera accessories and digital imaging software.

All right, put on your goggles and prepare to dissect your digital specimens. And boys, no flinging camera parts around the room or sticking cables up your noses, okay? Hey, that means you, mister!

Chapter 1

Filmless Fun, Facts, and Fiction

*I*f you've decided that the time is right to join the growing ranks of digital photographers, I'd like to offer a hearty "way to go!" — but also a word of caution. Before you hand over your money, be sure that you understand how this new technology works. Nothing's worse than a new toy that doesn't live up to your expectations. Remember how you felt when the plastic action figure that flew around the room in the TV commercial just stood there doing nothing after you dug it out of the cereal box? To make sure that you don't experience the same letdown with a digital camera, this chapter sorts out the facts from the fiction, explaining the pros and cons of digital imagery in general and digital cameras in particular.

Film? We Don't Need No Stinkin' Film!

Digital cameras come in all shapes and sizes. But although designs and features differ from model to model, all digital cameras are created to accomplish the same goal: to simplify the process of creating digital images.

When I speak of a *digital image,* I'm referring to a picture that you can view and edit on a computer. Digital images, like anything else on your computer screen, are nothing more than bits of electronic data. Your computer analyzes that data and displays the image on-screen. (For a detailed look at how digital images work, see Chapter 2.)

Digital images are nothing new — people have been creating and editing digital pictures using programs such as Adobe Photoshop and Corel PHOTO-PAINT for years. But until the advent of digital cameras, the process of getting a stunning sunset scene or an endearing baby picture into digital form required some time and effort. After shooting the picture with a film camera, you had to get the film developed and then have the photographic print or slide *digitized* (that is, converted to a computer image) using a piece of equipment known as a *scanner.* Assuming that you weren't well off enough to have a darkroom and a scanner in the east wing of your mansion, all this could take several days and involve several middlemen and associated middleman costs.

The film-and-scanner approach is still the most common way to create digital photographs. But digital cameras provide an easier, more convenient option. While traditional cameras capture images on film, digital cameras record what they see using computer chips and digital storage devices, creating images that can be immediately accessed by your computer. No film, film processing, or scanning is involved — you press the shutter button, and voilà: You have a digital image. To use the image, you simply transfer it from your camera to the computer, a process that can be accomplished in a variety of ways.

Fine, but Why Do I Want Digital Images?

Going digital opens up a world of artistic and practical possibilities that you simply don't enjoy with film. Here are just a few advantages of working with digital images:

> ✔ You gain added control over your pictures. With traditional photos, you have no input into an image after it leaves your camera. Everything rests in the hands of the

photofinisher. But with a digital photo, you can use your computer and photo-editing software to touch up your pictures, if necessary. You can correct contrast and colour-balance problems, improve focus, and cut unwanted objects from the scene.

Figures 1-1 and 1-2 illustrate the point: The top image shows an original digital photo. In addition to being overexposed, the picture is poorly framed and contains some distracting background elements. Parts of another swimmer's leg and foot are visible near the top of the frame, and some other unidentified object juts into the picture on the left.

I opened the picture in my photo editor and took care of all of these problems in a few minutes. I removed the intrusive background elements, adjusted the brightness and contrast, and cropped the picture to frame the main subject better. You can see the much-improved picture in Figure 1-2.

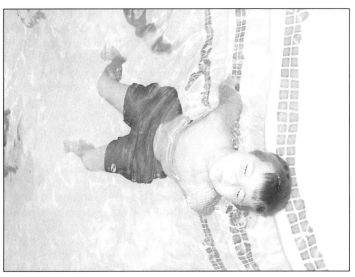

Figure 1-1: My original photo of this fledgling swimmer is overexposed and poorly framed.

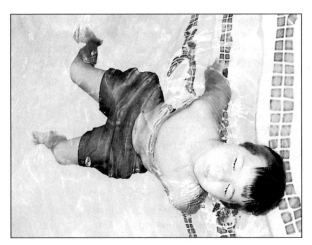

Figure 1-2: A little work in my photo editor turns a so-so image into a compelling summer memory.

Some would say that I could have created the same image with a film camera by paying attention to the background, exposure, and framing before I took the picture. But when you're photographing children and other fast-paced subjects, you have to shoot quickly. Had I taken the time to make sure that everything was perfect before I recorded the image, my opportunity to capture this subject would have been long gone. I'm not saying that you shouldn't strive to shoot the best pictures possible, but if something goes awry, you often can rescue marginal images in the editing stage.

✔ You can send an image to friends, family members, and clients almost instantaneously by attaching it to an e-mail message. Journalists covering stories in far-off lands can get pictures to their editors moments after snapping the images. Salespeople can send pictures of products to prospective buyers while the sales lead is still red-hot. Or, part-time antiques dealers can share finds with other dealers all over the world without leaving their homes.

Again, you can achieve the same thing with print photographs and the postal service — and don't think we don't all love receiving the 5 x 7 glossy of your dog wearing the Santa hat every Christmas. But if you had a digital image of Sparky, you could get the picture to all interested parties in a matter of minutes, not days. Not only is electronic distribution of images quicker than regular mail or overnight delivery services, it's also more convenient. You don't have to address an envelope, find a stamp, or truck off to the post office or delivery drop box.

✔ You can include pictures of your products, your office headquarters, or just your pretty face in multimedia presentations and on a Web site. Chapter 7 explains everything you need to do to prepare your images for both types of on-screen use.

✔ You can include digital images in business databases. For example, if your company operates a telemarketing program, you can insert images into a product order database so that when sales reps pull up information about a product, they see a picture of the product and can describe it to customers. Or you may want to insert product shots into inventory spreadsheets, as I did in Figure 1-3.

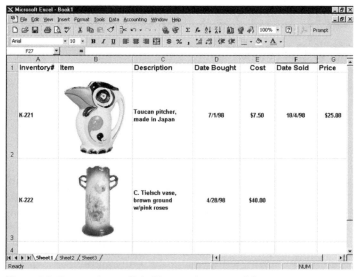

Figure 1-3: You can insert digital images into spreadsheets to create a visual inventory record.

✔ You can have fun exploring your artistic side. Using an image-editing program, you can apply wacky special effects, paint moustaches on your evil enemy, and otherwise distort reality.

> ✔ You can create your own personalized stationery, business cards, calendars, mugs, T-shirts, postcards, and other goodies, with one of many consumer image-editing programs that provides templates for creating such materials. You just select the design you want to use and insert your own photos into the template.
>
> After you place your photos into the templates, you can print your artwork on a colour printer using specialized print media sold by Kodak, Epson, Hewlett-Packard, and other vendors. If you don't have access to a printer with this capability, you can get the job done at a local photo centre or e-mail your image to one of the many vendors offering digital printing services via the Internet.

These are just some of the reasons digital imaging is catching on so quickly. For convenience, quality control, flexibility, and efficiency, digital does a slam-dunk on film.

But Can't I Do All This with a Scanner?

The answer to that question is, yes. You can do everything mentioned in the preceding section with any digital image, whether the picture comes from a scanner or a digital camera. However, digital cameras provide some benefits that you don't enjoy when you work with film prints and a scanner:

> ✔ If you're like most people, only a handful of pictures from every roll of film you have developed falls into the category of "that's a great picture" or even "that's an okay picture." Divide the cost of film and processing by the number of good photos per roll, and you'll discover that you're paying a lot more per picture than you thought.
>
> With a digital camera, you can review your pictures on your computer and then keep only those that are really special. Most cameras even have a built-in monitor that enables you to review your image immediately after you shoot the picture. If the picture isn't any good, you simply delete it from the computer or camera memory.

✔ Instant, on-camera review of your pictures also means added peace of mind when you're photographing one-time events such as an anniversary party or important business conference. You know right away whether you snapped a winner or need to try again. No more disappointing moments at the film lab when you discover that your packet of prints doesn't contain a single decent picture of the scene you wanted to capture.

✔ If you shoot product pictures on a regular basis, digital cameras offer significant time-savings. You don't have to run off to the lab and wait for your pictures to be processed.

✔ With some cameras, you can share your photos with a large group of people by hooking the camera up to a television monitor. You can even connect the camera to a VCR and make a videotape copy of all your images. Some cameras offer a slide-show mode that displays all the pictures in the camera's memory one by one, and a few cameras even enable you to record and play audio clips and text along with your pictures.

✔ Finally, digital cameras free up time that you would otherwise spend scanning pictures into your computer. Even the best scanners are painfully slow when compared with the time it takes to transfer pictures from a digital camera to the computer. To scan a single image on a top-of-the-line film scanner, for example, can take several minutes, especially if you want a high-resolution scan. In the same amount of time, you can transfer dozens of pictures from a camera to the computer.

In short, digital cameras save you time and money and, most important, make it easier to produce terrific pictures.

Now Tell Me the Downside

Thanks to design and manufacturing refinements, problems that kept people from moving to digital photography in the early days of the technology — high prices and questionable image quality being the most critical — have been solved. But a couple of downside issues remain, which I should bring up in the interest in fairness:

✔ Today's digital cameras can produce the same high quality prints as you've come to expect from your film camera. However, to enjoy that kind of picture quality, you need to start with a camera that offers moderate-to-high image resolution, which costs a minimum of $300. Images from lower-priced models just don't contain enough picture information to produce decent prints. Low-resolution cameras are fine for pictures that you want to use on a Web page or in a multimedia presentation, however. (See Chapter 2 for a complete explanation of resolution.)

✔ After you press the shutter button on a digital camera, the camera requires a few seconds to record the image to memory. During that time, you can't shoot another picture. With some cameras, you also experience a slight delay between the time you press the shutter button and the time the camera captures the image. These lag times can be a problem when you're trying to capture action-oriented events.

Generally speaking, the more expensive the camera, the less lag time you encounter. With some of the new, top-flight models, lag time isn't much more than you experience with a film camera using an automatic film advance.

Many digital cameras also offer a burst or continuous-capture mode that enables you to take a series of pictures with one press of the shutter button. This mode is helpful in some scenarios, although you're typically restricted to capturing images at a low resolution or without a flash. Chapter 5 provides more information.

✔ Becoming a digital photographer involves learning some new concepts and skills. If you're familiar with a computer, you shouldn't have much trouble getting up to speed with digital images. If you're a novice to both computers and digital cameras, expect to spend a fair amount of time making friends with your new machines. A digital camera may look and feel like your old film camera, but underneath the surface, it's a far cry from your father's Kodak Brownie. This book guides you through the process of becoming a digital photographer as painlessly as possible, but you need to invest the time to read the information it contains.

As manufacturers continue to refine digital-imaging technology, you can expect continued improvements in price and image-capture speed. I'm less hopeful that anything involving a computer will become easier to learn in the near future; my computer still forces me to "learn" something new every day — usually, the hard way. Of course, becoming proficient with film cameras requires some effort as well.

Whether or not digital will completely replace film as the foremost photographic medium remains to be seen. In all likelihood, digital and film will each secure their niche in the image world. So make a place for your new digital camera in your camera bag, but don't stick your film camera in the back of the closet just yet. Digital photography and film photography each offer unique advantages and disadvantages, and choosing one option to the exclusion of the other limits your creative flexibility.

Processing your digital images

In addition to the camera itself, digital photography involves some peripheral hardware and software, not the least of which is a fairly powerful computer for viewing, storing, editing, and printing your images. You need a machine with a robust processor, at least 64MB of RAM, and a big hard drive with lots of empty storage space. The least you can expect to spend on such a system is about $700.

In addition, you need to factor in the cost of image-editing software, image storage and transfer devices, camera batteries, and other peripherals. If you're a real photography buff, you may also want to buy special lenses, lights, a tripod, and some other accessories.

Nope, a digital darkroom isn't cheap. Then again, neither is traditional film photography, if you're a serious photographer. And when you consider all the benefits of digital imagery, especially if you do business nationally or internationally, justifying the expense isn't all that difficult. But just in case you're getting queasy, look in Chapter 3 for more details on the various components involved in digital photography — plus some tips on how to cut budgetary corners.

Chapter 2

Mr. Science Explains It All

● ●

In This Chapter

▶ Understanding how digital cameras record images

▶ Perusing a perfectly painless primer on pixels

▶ Exploring the murky waters of resolution

▶ Analyzing the undying relationship between resolution and image size

▶ Looking at f-stops, shutter speeds, and other aspects of image exposure

● ●

*I*f discussions of a technical nature make you nauseated, keep a stomach-soothing potion handy while you read this chapter. The following pages are full of the kind of technical babble that makes science teachers drool but leaves us ordinary mortals feeling motion sick.

Unfortunately, you can't be a successful digital photographer without getting acquainted with the science behind the art. But never fear: This chapter provides you with the ideal lab partner as you explore such important concepts as pixels, resolution, f-stops, and more. Sorry, you don't dissect pond creatures or analyze the cell structure of your fingernails in this science class, but you do get to peel back the skin of a digital camera and examine the guts of a digital image. Neither exercise is for the faint of heart, but both are critical for understanding how to turn out quality images.

From Your Eyes to the Camera's Memory

A traditional camera creates an image by allowing light to pass through a lens onto film. The film is coated with light-sensitive chemicals, and wherever light hits the coating, a chemical reaction takes place, recording a latent image. During the film development stage, more chemicals transform the latent image into a printed photograph.

Digital cameras also use light to create images, but instead of film, digital cameras capture pictures using an *imaging array,* which is a fancy way of saying "light-sensitive computer chips." Currently, these chips come in two flavours: CCD, which stands for *charge-coupled device,* and CMOS, which is short for *complementary metal-oxide semiconductor.* (No, Billy, that information won't be on the test.)

Although CCD and CMOS chips differ in some important ways, both chips do essentially the same thing. When struck by light, they emit an electrical charge, which is analyzed and translated into digital image data by a processor inside the camera. The more light, the stronger the charge.

After the electrical impulses are converted to image data, the data is saved to the camera's memory, which may come in the form of an in-camera chip or a removable memory card or disk. To access the images that your camera records, you just transfer them from the camera memory to your computer. With some cameras, you can transfer pictures directly to a television monitor or printer, enabling you to view and print your photographs without ever turning on your computer.

Keep in mind that what you've just read is only a basic explanation of how digital cameras record images. I could write an entire chapter on CCD designs, for example, but you would only wind up with a big headache.

Resolution Rules!

Without a doubt, the number one thing you can do to improve your digital photos is to understand the concept of *resolution.* Unless you make the right choices about resolution, your pictures will be a disappointment, no matter how captivating the subject. In other words, don't skip this section!

Pixels: The building blocks of every digital photo

Have you ever seen the painting *A Sunday Afternoon on the Island of La Grande Jatte,* by the French artist Georges Seurat? Seurat was a master of a technique known as *pointillism,* in which scenes are composed of millions of tiny dots of paint, created by dabbing the canvas with the tip of a paintbrush. When you stand across the room from a pointillist painting, the dots blend together, forming a seamless image. Only when you get up close to the canvas can you distinguish the individual dots.

Digital images work something like pointillist paintings. Rather than being made up of dots of paint, however, digital images are composed of tiny squares of colour known as *pixels.* The term *pixel* is short for *picture element.* Don't you wish you could get a job thinking up these clever computer words?

If you magnify an image on-screen, you can make out the individual pixels, as shown in Figure 2-1. Zoom out on the image, and the pixels seem to blend together, just as when you step back from a pointillist painting.

Every digital photograph is born with a set number of pixels, which you control by using the capture settings on your digital camera. Low-end digital cameras typically create images that are 640 pixels wide and 480 pixels tall. More expensive models can produce images with many more pixels and also enable you to record images at a variety of capture settings, each of which results in a different pixel count. (See Chapter 5 for details on this step in the picture-taking process.)

Some people use the term *pixel dimensions* to refer to the number of pixels in an image — number of pixels wide by number of pixels high. Others use the term *image size,* which can lead to confusion because that term is also used to refer to the physical dimensions of the picture when printed (inches wide by inches tall, for example). For the record, I use *pixel dimensions* to refer specifically to the pixel count and *image size* or *print size* to mean the print dimensions.

Figure 2-1: Zooming in on a digital photo enables you to see the individual pixels.

Image resolution and print quality

Before you print an image, you use a control in your photo editor to specify an *output resolution,* which determines the number of pixels per inch (ppi). This value, which many people refer to as simply *resolution,* has a major effect on the quality of your printed digital photos.

The more pixels per inch, the crisper the picture. A digital photo with an output resolution of 300 ppi looks crisp and terrific. When the output resolution of that same image is reduced to 150 ppi, the picture loses some sharpness and detail. Reducing the output resolution to 75 ppi results in significant image degradation.

Note that output resolution is measured in terms of pixels per *linear* inch, not square inch. So a resolution of 75 ppi means that you have 75 pixels horizontally and 75 pixels vertically, or 5625 pixels for each square inch of image.

Why does the 75-ppi image look so much worse than its higher-resolution counterparts? Because at 75 ppi, the pixels are bigger. After all, if you divide an inch into 75 squares, the squares are significantly larger than if you divide the inch into 150 squares or 300 squares. And the bigger the pixel, the easier it is for your eye to figure out that it's really just looking at a bunch of squares. Areas that contain diagonal and curved lines, such as the edges of a coin or handwritten lettering, take on a stair-stepped appearance.

Image resolution and on-screen picture quality

Although output resolution — pixels per inch — has a dramatic effect on the quality of printed photos, it's a moot point for pictures displayed on-screen. A computer monitor (or other screen device) cares only about the pixel dimensions, not pixels per inch, despite what you may have been told by some folks. The number of pixels does control the *size* at which the picture appears on the monitor, however.

Like digital cameras, computer monitors create everything you see on-screen out of pixels. You typically can choose from several monitor settings, each of which results in a different number of screen pixels. Standard settings include 640 x 480 pixels, 800 x 600 pixels, and 1024 x 768 pixels.

When you display a digital photo on your computer monitor, the monitor completely ignores output resolution (ppi) and simply devotes one screen pixel to every image pixel. So if you set your digital camera to record a 640 x 480-pixel image, that picture consumes the whole screen on a monitor that's set to the 640 x 480 display setting.

This fact is great news for digital photographers with low budgets, because even the most inexpensive digital camera captures enough pixels to cover a large expanse of on-screen real estate. (Read "More mind-boggling resolution stuff," later in this chapter, for more information about screen display;

also, refer to Chapter 7 for specifics on how to size your images for the screen.)

How many pixels are enough?

Because printers and screen devices think about pixels differently, your pixel needs vary depending on how you plan to use your picture.

- ✔ If you want to use your picture on a Web page or for some other on-screen use, you need very few pixels. As explained in the preceding section, you just need to match the pixel dimensions of the picture to the amount of the screen you want the image to fill. In most cases, 640 x 480 pixels is more than enough, and for many projects, half that many pixels or even fewer will do.

- ✔ If you plan to print your photo and want the best picture quality, you need enough pixels to enable you to set the output resolution in the neighbourhood of 200 to 300 ppi. This number varies depending on the printer; sometimes you can get by with fewer pixels. Check your printer manual for precise resolution guidelines.

To determine the maximum size at which you can print a picture at a particular resolution, just divide the total number of horizontal image pixels by the desired resolution. Or divide the total number of vertical pixels by the desired resolution. Say that your camera captures 1280 pixels horizontally and 960 pixels vertically. If your target resolution is 300 ppi, divide 1280 by 300 to get the maximum image width — in this case, about 4.25 inches. Or to find out the maximum height, divide 960 by 300, which equals about 3.25 inches. So you can print a 4.25 x 3.25-inch image at 300 ppi.

Because I've hammered home the point that more pixels means better print quality, you may think that if 300 ppi delivers good print quality, higher resolutions produce even better quality. But this isn't the case. In fact, exceeding that 300-ppi ceiling can degrade image quality. Printers are engineered to work with images set to a particular resolution, and when presented with an image file at a higher resolution, most printers simply eliminate the extra pixels. Printers don't always do a great job of slimming down the pixel population, and the result can be muddy or jagged photos. You get better results if you do the job yourself in your photo-editing software.

If you're not sure how you're going to use your digital photos, set your camera to the setting that's appropriate for print pictures. If you later want to use a picture on a Web page or for some other on-screen use, you can delete extra pixels as necessary. But you can't rely on being able to add pixels after the fact with any degree of success. For more about this subject, see the upcoming section "So how do I control pixels and output resolution?"

More pixels means bigger files

Each pixel in a digital photo adds to the size of the image file. For example, an image that measures 1110 pixels wide and 725 pixels tall has a total pixel count of 804,750. This file consumes roughly 2.3MB (megabytes) of storage space. Some of that file space is dedicated to colour data, however. The greyscale version of the picture contains the same number of pixels as its full-colour cousin but has a file size of about 790K (kilobytes).

By contrast, a 75-ppi version of the same image measures 278 pixels wide by 181 pixels tall, for a total of 50,318 pixels. The full-colour version of this image has a file size of just 153K; the greyscale version, 55K.

In addition to eating up storage space, large image files make big demands on your computer's memory (RAM) when you edit them. Typically, the RAM requirement is roughly three times the file size. And when placed on a Web page, huge image files are a major annoyance. Every kilobyte increases the time required to download the file.

To avoid straining your computer — and the patience of Web site visitors — keep your images lean and mean. You want the appropriate number of pixels to suit your final output device (screen or printer), but no more. You can read about designing pictures for screen use in Chapter 7.

So how do I control pixels and output resolution?

Every digital photo starts out with a set number of pixels, which is determined by the capture setting you use when you shoot the picture. When you open a picture in your photo editor, the software assigns a default output resolution, which is typically either 75 ppi or 300 ppi. To prepare your picture for printing or on-screen use, you may need to adjust the output resolution or the pixel dimensions. The next two sections introduce you to different approaches to this task.

Adding and deleting pixels (resampling)

One way to increase or decrease output resolution — in other words, to change the number of pixels per inch — is to add or delete pixels with your image-editing software, a process known as *resampling*. Image-editing gurus refer to the process of adding pixels as *upsampling*, and deleting pixels as *downsampling*. When you add or delete pixels, you're changing the pixel dimensions of the image.

Upsampling sounds like a good idea — if you don't have enough pixels, you just go to the Pixel Mart and fill your basket, right? The problem is that when you add pixels, the image-editing software simply makes its best guess as to what colour and brightness to make the new pixels. And even high-end image-editing programs don't do a very good job of pulling pixels out of thin air.

With some images, you can get away with minimal upsampling — say, 10 to 15 percent — but with other images, you notice a quality loss with even slight pixel infusions. Images with large, flat areas of colour tend to survive upsampling better than pictures with lots of intricate details.

If your image contains too many pixels, which is often the case for pictures that you want to use on the Web, you can safely delete pixels (downsample). But keep in mind that every pixel you throw away contains image information, so too much pixel-dumping can degrade image quality. Try not to downsample by more than 25 percent, and always make a backup copy of your image in case you ever want those original pixels back.

For tips on how to alter your pixel count, see the section related to sizing images for on-screen display in Chapter 7.

Resizing: The better way to adjust output resolution

A better way to change the output resolution is to resize the image *while maintaining the original pixel count.* If you reduce the print size of the image, the pixels shrink and move closer together in order to fit into their new boundaries. If you enlarge the print size, the pixels puff themselves up and spread out to fill in the expanded image area.

Say that you have a 4 x 3-inch image set to an output resolution of 150 ppi. If you double the image size, to 8 x 6 inches, the resolution is cut in half, to 75 ppi. Naturally, the lower output resolution reduces your print quality, for reasons explained earlier in this chapter (see "Image resolution and print quality"). Conversely, if you reduce the image size by half, to 2 x 1.5 inches, the output resolution is doubled, to 300 ppi, and your print quality should improve.

Not all image-editing programs enable you to maintain your original pixel count when resizing images. Programs that don't provide this option typically automatically resample your image whenever you resize your photo, so be careful. Check your program's help system or manual to get details on your resizing and resolution controls. If you don't find any specific information, you can test the program by making a copy of a picture and then enlarging the copy. If the file size of the enlarged picture is bigger than the file size of the original, the program added pixels to your image.

More mind-boggling resolution stuff

As if sorting out all the pixel, resampling, and resolution stuff discussed in the preceding sections isn't challenging enough, you also need to be aware that *resolution* doesn't always refer to output resolution as just described. The term is also used to describe the capabilities of digital cameras, monitors, and scanners. So when you hear the word *resolution,* keep the following distinctions in mind:

 ✔ **Camera resolution:** Digital camera manufacturers often use the term *resolution* to describe the number of pixels in the pictures produced by their cameras. A camera's stated resolution may be 640 x 480 pixels or 1.3 million pixels, for example. But those values refer to the pixel dimensions or total pixels a camera can produce, not the number of pixels per inch in the final image. *You* determine that value in your photo-editing software. Of course, you can use the camera's pixel count to figure out the final resolution you can achieve from your images, as described earlier in "How many pixels are enough?"

Some vendors use the term *VGA resolution* to indicate a 640 x 480-pixel image, *XGA resolution* to indicate a 1024 x 768-pixel image, and *megapixel resolution* to indicate a total pixel count of 1 million or more.

✔ **Monitor resolution:** Manufacturers of computer monitors also use the word *resolution* to describe the number of pixels a monitor can display. Most monitors enable you to choose from display settings of 640 x 480 pixels (again, often referred to as VGA resolution), 800 x 600 pixels, or 1024 x 768 pixels (XGA). Some monitors can display even more pixels.

See Chapter 7 to get more details about how screen resolution relates to image resolution.

✔ **Scanner resolution:** Scanner resolution is usually stated in the same terms as image resolution, thankfully. A low-end scanner typically captures a maximum of 600 pixels per inch.

By the way, if you're scanner shopping, pay attention to *optical resolution,* which is a scanner's "real" resolution. Many scanner models make a big deal about offering a high *interpolated* or *enhanced* resolution, but that higher resolution is the result of upsampling from the model's optical (true) resolution. If the importance of that fact is lost on you, read the section, "Adding and deleting pixels (resampling)," earlier in this chapter. Or just remember this: The optical resolution is the important measure of a scanner's capabilities.

What all this resolution stuff means to you

Head starting to hurt? Mine, too. So to help you sort out all the information you accumulated by reading the preceding sections, here's a brief summary of resolution matters that matter most:

✔ **Number of pixels across (or down) ÷ printed image width (or height) = output resolution (ppi).** For example, 600 pixels divided by 2 inches equals 300 ppi.

✔ **For good-quality prints, you typically need an output resolution of 200 to 300 ppi.**

✔ **For on-screen display, think in terms of pixel dimensions, not output resolution.**

✔ **Enlarging a print can reduce image quality.** When you enlarge an image, one of two things has to happen. Either the existing pixels expand to fit the new image boundaries, or the pixels stay the same size and the image-editing software adds pixels to fill in the gaps. Either way, your image quality can suffer.

✔ **To safely raise the output resolution of an existing image, reduce the print size.** Again, adding pixels to raise the output resolution rarely delivers good results. Instead, retain the existing number of pixels and reduce the print dimensions of the picture.

✔ **Set your camera to capture a pixel count at or above what you need for your final picture output.** Most cameras enable you to capture images at several different pixel dimensions. Remember that you can safely toss away pixels if you want a lower image resolution later, but you can't add pixels without risking damage to your image. Also, you may need a low-resolution image today — for example, if you want to display a picture on the Web — but you may decide later that you want to print the image at a larger size, in which case you're going to need those extra pixels. For more on this issue, see Chapter 5.

✔ **Increasing pixels means a bigger image file.** And even if you have tons of file-storage space to hold all those huge images, bigger isn't always better. Large images require a ton of RAM to edit and increase the time your photo software needs to process your edits. On a Web page, large image files mean long download times. Finally, sending more pixels to the printer than are needed often produces worse, not better, prints. If your image has a higher resolution than required by the output device (printer or monitor), see Chapter 7 for information on how to dump the excess pixels.

Lights, Camera, Exposure!

Whether you're working with a digital camera or a traditional film camera, the brightness or darkness of the image is dependent on *exposure* — the amount of light that hits the film or image-sensor array. The more light, the brighter the image. Too much light results in a washed-out, or *overexposed,* image; too little light, and the image is dark, or *underexposed.*

Most low-to-medium priced digital cameras, like point-and-shoot film cameras, don't give you much control over exposure; everything is handled automatically for you. But some cameras offer a choice of automatic exposure settings, and higher-end cameras provide manual exposure control.

Regardless of whether you're shooting with an automatic model or one that offers manual controls, you should be aware of the different factors that affect exposure — including shutter speed, aperture, and ISO rating — so that you can understand the limitations and possibilities of your camera.

Aperture, f-stops, and shutter speeds: The traditional way

Before taking a look at how digital cameras control exposure, it helps to understand how a film camera does the job. Even though digital cameras don't function in quite the same way as film cameras, manufacturers describe their exposure control mechanisms using traditional film terms, hoping to make the transition from film to digital easier for experienced photographers.

Figure 2-2 shows a simplified illustration of a film camera. Although the specific component design varies depending on the type of camera, all film cameras include some sort of shutter, which is placed between the film and the lens. When the camera isn't in use, the shutter is closed, preventing light from reaching the film. When you take a picture, the shutter opens, and light hits the film. (Now you know why the little button you press to take a picture is called the *shutter button* and why people who take lots of pictures are called *shutterbugs.)*

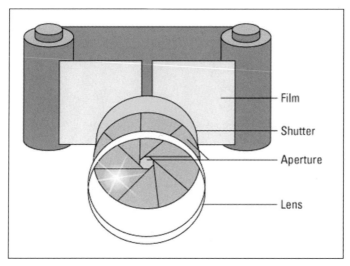

Figure 2-2: A look at the shutter and aperture in a traditional film camera.

You can control the amount of light that reaches the film in two ways: by adjusting the amount of time the shutter stays open (referred to as the *shutter speed*) and by changing the *aperture*. The aperture, labelled in Figure 2-2, is a hole in an adjustable diaphragm set between the lens and the shutter. Light coming through the lens is funnelled through this hole to the shutter and then onto the film. So if you want more light to strike the film, you make the aperture bigger; if you want less light, you make the aperture smaller.

The size of the aperture opening is measured in f-numbers, more commonly referred to as *f-stops*. Standard aperture settings are f/1.4, f/2, f/2.8, f/4, f/5.6, f/8, f/11, f/16, and f/22.

Contrary to what you may expect, the larger the f-stop number, the smaller the aperture and the less light that enters the camera. Each f-stop setting lets in half as much light as the next smaller f-stop number. For example, the camera gets twice as much light at f/11 as it does at f/16. (And here you were complaining that computers were confusing!) See Figure 2-3 for an illustration that may help you get a grip on f-stops.

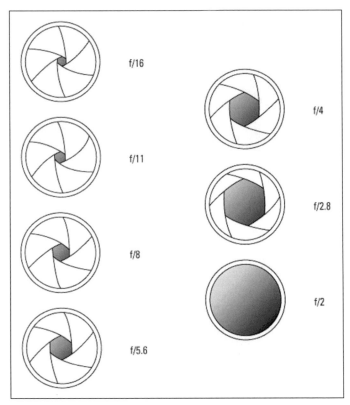

Figure 2-3: As the f-stop number decreases, the aperture size grows and more light enters the camera.

Shutter speeds are measured in more obvious terms: fractions of a second. A shutter speed of 1/8, for example, means that the shutter opens for one-eighth of a second. That may not sound like much time, but in camera years, it's in fact a very long period. Try to capture a moving object at that speed and you wind up with a big blur. You need a shutter speed of about 1/500 to capture action clearly.

On cameras that offer aperture and shutter-speed control, you manipulate the two settings in tandem to capture just the right amount of light. For example, if you are capturing fast action on a bright, sunny day, you can combine a fast shutter speed with a small aperture (high f-stop number). To shoot the same picture at twilight, you need a wide-open aperture (small f-stop number) in order to use the same fast shutter speed.

Aperture, shutter speed, and f-stops: The digital way

As with a film camera, the exposure of a picture shot with a digital camera depends on the amount of light that the camera captures. But some digital cameras don't use a traditional shutter/aperture arrangement to control exposure. Instead, the chips in the image-sensor array simply turn on and off for different periods of time, thereby capturing more or less light. In some cameras, exposure is also varied — either automatically or by some control the user sets — by boosting or reducing the strength of the electrical charge that a chip emits in response to a certain amount of light.

Even on cameras that use this alternative approach to exposure control, the camera's capabilities are usually stated in traditional film-camera terms. For example, you may have a choice of two exposure settings, which may be labelled with icons that look like the aperture openings shown in Figure 2-3. The settings are engineered to deliver the *equivalent* exposure that you would get with a film camera using the same f-stop.

Aperture and shutter speeds aren't the only factors involved in image exposure, however. The sensitivity of the image-sensor array also plays a role, as explained next.

ISO ratings and chip sensitivity

Pick up a box of film, and you should see an *ISO number.* This number tells you how sensitive the film is to light and is also referred to as the *film speed.*

Film geared to the consumer market typically offers ratings of ISO 100, 200, or 400. The higher the number, the more sensitive the film, or, if you prefer photography lingo, the *faster* the film. And the faster the film, the less light you need to capture a decent image. The advantage of using a faster film is that you can use a faster shutter speed and shoot in dimmer lighting than you can with a low-speed film. On the downside, photos shot with fast film sometimes exhibit noticeable *grain* — that is, they have a slightly speckled appearance.

Most digital camera manufacturers also provide an ISO rating for their cameras. This number tells you the *equivalent* sensitivity of the chips on the image-sensor array. In other words, the value reflects the speed of film you'd be using if you were using a traditional camera rather than a digital camera. Typically, consumer-model digital cameras have an equivalency of about ISO 100–400.

I bring all this up because it explains why digital cameras need so much light to produce a decent image. If you were really shooting with ISO 100 film, you would need a wide-open aperture or a slow shutter speed to capture an image in low lighting — assuming that you weren't aiming for the ghostly-shapes-in-a-dimly-lit-cave effect on purpose. The same is true of digital cameras.

Some digital cameras enable you to choose from a few different ISO settings. Unfortunately, raising the ISO setting simply boosts the electronic signal that's produced when you snap a picture. Although this does permit a faster shutter speed, the extra signal power results in electronic "noise" that leads to grainy pictures, just as you get with fast film. With digital cameras, though, you'll notice even more grain than with the equivalent film ISO. Most camera manuals suggest using the lowest ISO setting for best quality — as do I.

Chapter 4 discusses this example and other exposure issues in more detail.

Chapter 3

Extra Goodies for Extra Fun

● ●

In This Chapter

▶ Buying and using removable storage media

▶ Transferring images to your computer the easy way

▶ Printing your images

▶ Choosing a digital closet (storage solutions)

▶ Seeking out the best imaging software

▶ Stabilizing and lighting your shots

▶ Protecting your camera from death and destruction

● ●

Do you remember your first Barbie doll or — if you're a guy who refuses to admit playing with a girl's toy — your first G.I. Joe? In and of themselves, the dolls were entertaining enough, especially if the adult who ruled your household didn't get too upset when you tried stuff like shaving Barbie's head and finding out whether G.I. Joe could withstand a spin in the garbage disposal. But Barbie and Joe were even more fun if you could talk some doting adult into buying you some of the many doll accessories on the toy-store shelves. With a few changes of clothing, a plastic convertible or tank, and loyal doll friends like Midge and Ken, Dollworld was a much more interesting place.

Similarly, you can enhance your digital photography experience by adding a few hardware and software accessories. Digital camera accessories don't bring quite the same rush as a Barbie penthouse or a G.I. Joe surface-to-air missile, but they greatly expand your creative options and make some aspects of digital photography easier.

This chapter introduces you to some of the best camera accessories, from adapters that speed the process of downloading images, to software that enables you to retouch and otherwise manipulate your photographs.

Memory Cards and Other Camera Media

If your camera stores pictures on removable storage media, you may have received one memory card or disk with your camera. At a minimum, cameras that include removable media in the box typically provide at least 8MB of storage capacity.

In the days when digital cameras produced only low-resolution images, 8MB was more storage space than most people needed on a regular basis. But because today's models can capture many more pixels than cameras even a few years old, 8MB now represents just a starting point for most digital photographers.

How much storage space do you need? That depends on how many pictures you want to take at a time and what resolution and compression settings you use when you shoot those images. Your camera manual should provide a table that lists the file sizes of pictures taken at each of the resolution and compression settings the camera offers. Use these numbers as a guide to how many megabytes of storage will serve your needs.

If you can get by with fewer pixels or you don't mind applying a high degree of compression to your photos, your memory needs will be much smaller because the image files are smaller. And of course, if you usually have a computer close by, enabling you to download images when you fill up your existing memory, you may not need any additional memory at all.

After you decide on how many megabytes you need, look to the following sections for everything you need to know about buying and caring for your storage media.

Field guide to camera memory

Removable media for digital cameras comes in several flavours. Most digital cameras can use only one type, however, so check your manual to find out which of the following options works with your model. For a look at the most common types of removable camera memory, see Figure 3-1. The options in the top row, a mini-CD and standard floppy disk, are used by some Sony digital cameras, as is the Memory Stick in the bottom row. Most other manufacturers design their cameras around either SmartMedia or CompactFlash cards, also shown in the bottom row. A few new cameras, especially those that feature tiny camera bodies, store pictures on the diminutive Secure Digital (SD) cards.

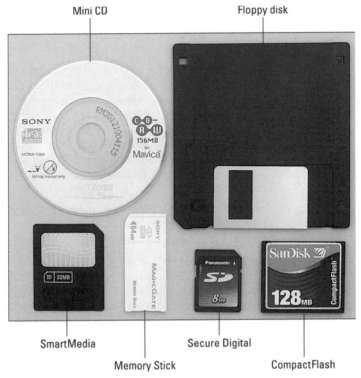

Figure 3-1: Digital cameras store pictures on a variety of removable media.

Note that in the descriptions here, prices are what you can expect to pay in retail or online stores — what the trade refers to as "street prices." Fortunately, prices have fallen recently, while storage capacities seem to be ever increasing. So by the time you read this, you may be able to get even more for your money.

> ✔ **Floppy disks:** Some Digital Mavica cameras from Sony store images on regular old floppy disks. If you own one of these models, purchasing additional memory is a no-brainer; floppy disks are pennies apiece, so stock up. Remember that each floppy can hold less than 1.5MB of image data.

✔ **PC Cards:** Some professional-level digital cameras, as well as a few older models of consumer cameras, accept PC Cards, formally known as PCMCIA Cards. About the size of a credit card, these memory cards are the same type used by most laptop computers. If your camera uses PC Cards, be sure to find out whether it uses Type I, II, or III before going shopping. Prices for PC Card memory range from about $1 to $2 per megabyte, depending on the type and capacity of the card.

✔ **CompactFlash:** Smaller versions of PC Cards, CompactFlash cards sport a hard-shell outer case and pin connectors at one end. These cards come in two flavours: Type I and the slightly thicker Type II. Cameras that accept Type II cards typically can also read Type I cards, but the reverse isn't true unless you use an adapter. Currently, you can buy cards in capacities ranging from 8MB to 1GB (gigabyte). Both Type I and Type II cards range from $.50 to $1 per megabyte.

✔ **SmartMedia:** These cards are smaller, thinner, and more flexible than CompactFlash cards; they feel sort of like the old 5.25-inch floppy disks from the dark ages of computing.

You sometimes see the initials *SSFDC* in conjunction with the SmartMedia moniker. SSFDC stands for Solid State Floppy Disk Card and refers to the technology used in the cards. But if you go into a store and ask for an SSFDC card, you're likely to be greeted by blank stares, so stick with SmartMedia instead.

Like CompactFlash cards, SmartMedia cards come in several different capacities, but the biggest-capacity SmartMedia card you can buy at present is 128MB. You'll pay about $.50 to $1 per megabyte, and, as with most memory cards, you get a better per-megabyte price if you buy the larger-capacity cards.

SmartMedia cards are made in two different voltages, 3.3 volts and 5 volts, to accommodate different types of cameras. Check your camera's manual to find out which voltage you need. Also be aware that a few older digital cameras can't use the highest capacity SmartMedia cards.

✔ **Sony Memory Stick:** This type of memory card works only with certain Sony digital cameras and other Sony devices. The largest capacity Memory Stick card holds 128MB of data. Cost per megabyte is about the same as for CompactFlash and SmartMedia cards.

✔ **And the rest:** I lump these last storage options together because only a handful of cameras use them:

- **Secure Digital (SD):** Some of the newest digital cameras store pictures on SD cards, a relatively new type of memory card that's about the size of a postage stamp. These cards come in capacities up to 128MB and cost about $1 to $2 per megabyte.

- **IBM Microdrive:** Some high-resolution cameras can store images on an IBM Microdrive as well as CompactFlash Type I and Type II cards. The Microdrive, which is about the same physical size as a CompactFlash card, comes in capacities from 340MB to 1GB.

- **Mini CD-R:** Sony offers high-resolution Mavica models that store images on miniature CDs. About three inches in diameter, these discs can store 156MB of data. Some of the cameras feature CD-R technology, while others offer both CD-R and CD-RW. (With CD-R, you can't erase images once they're on the CD. See the sidebar "CD-R or CD-RW?" elsewhere in this chapter for more information.)

Prices for all types of removable media vary quite a bit depending on where you buy and what brand you buy. So shop around — you likely can get even better prices than mentioned here if you watch the sale ads. Also, many stores offer extra memory as a bonus when you buy a particular camera, so keep an eye out for these promotions if you're camera shopping.

Care and feeding of CompactFlash and SmartMedia cards

CompactFlash and SmartMedia cards are the most widely used types of removable camera memory. Although the cost of both products has dropped dramatically over the past year, you can easily spend as much on them as you do for a camera if you buy a couple of large capacity cards. To protect your investment — as well as the images that you store on the cards — pay attention to the following care and maintenance tips:

✔ When you insert a memory card into your camera for the first time, you may need to format the card so that it's prepared to accept your digital images. Your camera should have a format procedure, so check your manual.

✔ Never remove the card while the camera is still recording or accessing the data on the card. (Most cameras display a little light or indicator to let you know when the card is in use.)

✔ Don't turn off the power to your camera while the camera is accessing the card, either.

✔ Avoid touching the contact areas of the card.

  • On a SmartMedia card, the gold region at the top of the card is the no-touch zone.

  • On a CompactFlash card, keep your mitts off the connector on the bottom of the card.

✔ Don't bend a SmartMedia card. SmartMedia cards are flexible, so if you decide to carry them in your hip pocket, don't sit down.

✔ If your card gets dirty, wipe it clean with a soft, dry cloth. Dirt and grime can affect the performance of memory cards.

✔ Try not to expose memory cards to heat, humidity, static electricity, and strong electrical noise. You don't need to be overly paranoid, but use some common sense in this area.

✔ Ignore those rumours you hear about airport security scanners destroying data on memory cards. This rumour has become a hot one again with the installation of newer, stronger scanners in some airports. But according to manufacturers of storage cards, security scanners do no harm to the cards. So instead of worrying about your data being damaged when you put your camera bag through the scanner, keep an eye out for airport thieves who would like nothing more than to lift your camera off the scanner belt while you're not paying attention.

Download Devices

In years past, most digital cameras came with a serial cable for connecting the camera to the computer. To download images, you plugged the cable into both devices and used special image-transfer software to move the pictures from camera to computer. This method of file transfer was excruciatingly slow — transferring a dozen pictures could easily take 20 minutes or more.

Thankfully, most manufacturers have now switched over to USB technology for image transfer. In case you're wondering, USB stands for *Universal Serial Bus* and is the geeky name assigned to a type of connection between two digital devices — in this case, camera and computer. Most cameras ship with a USB cable that works on both Windows-based and Macintosh computers that have USB ports.

With USB, images flow from camera to computer much more quickly than via serial cable. But USB presents two problems. First, if your computer is a few years old, your machine may not have a USB port to connect to. And if you use Windows 95 as your computer's operating system, expect a hassle getting USB connections to work, even if you install the updated version of Windows 95 that supposedly corrects USB hang-ups.

The difficulties presented by direct camera-to-computer connections helped the Sony Digital Mavica cameras that store images on floppy disk become huge sellers. With these models, you don't have to mess with getting camera and computer to shake hands through a cable. You just eject the floppy disk from the camera and push it into your computer's floppy disk drive to download images.

Similarly, CD Mavica cameras store pictures on miniature CD-R and CD-RW disks that you slip into your computer's CD-ROM drive to transfer images. With some computers, a supplied adapter is necessary in order to make the CDs work in the CD drive. Figure 3-2 shows a CD Mavica model along with the adapter.

Figure 3-2: An adapter supplied with Sony CD Mavica cameras makes image data readable by CD-ROM drives that can't normally open files stored on miniature CDs.

In the past few years, manufacturers have developed devices that enable photographers whose cameras use other types of removable storage media to enjoy the same download speed and convenience offered by the Mavica's floppy-disk set-up. If you shoot digitally on a regular basis, you definitely should get one of these gadgets — you'll never regret the investment. Not only can you transfer images to your computer in a flash, you save yourself the annoyance of fiddling with cable connections between your computer and camera every time you want to download some images. Here's a look at your options:

 ✔ **Floppy disk adapter:** For about $60, you can buy an adapter that makes SmartMedia and Memory Stick cards readable by your floppy disk drive. Figure 3-3 shows an adapter that works with SmartMedia cards. With either type of card, you just slip the card into the adapter and then put the adapter into your floppy drive. You can then drag and drop image files from the floppy drive to your hard drive as you would any file on a floppy disk.

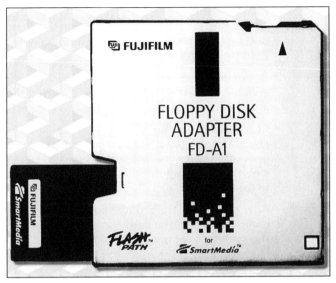

Figure 3-3: A floppy disk adapter enables you to transfer pictures from a SmartMedia card via your computer's floppy disk drive.

✔ **PC Card adapter:** These adapters enable CompactFlash, SmartMedia, Secure Digital, and Memory Stick cards to masquerade as standard PC Cards. You can also buy an adapter for the IBM Microdrive.

Figure 3-4 offers a glimpse of an adapter for a CompactFlash card. After putting the memory card in the adapter, you insert the whole shebang into your laptop computer's PC

Figure 3-4: This adapter makes CompactFlash cards readable in PC Card slots, which are found on many laptop computers.

Card slot or into a PC Card reader (see the next bullet point). The PC Card shows up as a drive on your computer desktop, and you drag and drop image files from the PC Card to your hard drive.

Some CompactFlash manufacturers provide a free PC Card adapter when you buy a memory card, but the adapters are also available independently for about $10.

✔ **Card reader:** Another download alternative for easy image transfer is a memory-card reader. You can buy an internal card reader that installs into an empty expansion slot on your computer or an external reader that cables to the computer, usually via a parallel port or USB port.

After you install the reader's driver software, your computer "sees" the card reader as just another drive on the system, like your floppy drive or your hard drive. You insert your memory card into the reader and then drag and drop the files from the reader to your hard drive.

You can buy card readers that accept a single type of memory card for about $25, but for added flexibility and long-term functionality, you may want to invest a little more and get a multi-format reader such as the Microtech USB CameraMate. This reader, shown on the right side of Figure 3-5, can transfer files from an IBM Microdrive as well as CompactFlash and SmartMedia cards. (Some versions of this product also accept Memory Stick cards.) If you buy a camera down the road and the camera uses different media than your old one, you won't need to buy a new card reader. You also can download images taken by visitors whose cameras use different media than yours.

If you buy a card reader that connects via the parallel port, look for a model that offers a *pass-through connection* for your printer. In plain English, that means that you connect the reader to the parallel port and then connect the printer to the reader. That way, the two devices can share the same parallel port, which is important because many computers have only one parallel port. But be advised that some printers aren't happy with this arrangement and may spit out garbage pages every now and then to voice their displeasure. Before buying a card reader (or any other device, for that matter) that provides a pass-through connection, pay a visit to the manufacturer's Web site and check for any potential hardware conflicts.

Figure 3-5: To transfer images from a memory card via USB, you can use devices such as the Microtech USB CameraMate (front right) and the Lexar Media JumpShot cable, shown here plugged into a laptop computer (front left).

Another USB option, the Lexar Media JumpShot cable, shown on the left side of Figure 3-5, enables you to transfer images from USB-enabled CompactFlash cards, also from Lexar Media. Technically, the JumpShot cable (about $20) isn't a card reader — functions normally handled by the reader are built into the card itself, and the cable just serves to connect the card to the computer. But together, the card and cable work like a card reader, so don't worry about the specifics. The USB-enabled cards fall into the same price range as ordinary CompactFlash cards and work in any device that accepts CompactFlash media. You can't use regular CompactFlash cards with the JumpShot cable, however.

✔ **Docking stations:** Because so many new users have trouble with the process of downloading images from camera to computer — no, you're *not* the only one! — a few manufacturers have developed so-called *camera docks* that are designed to simplify things. A dock is a small base unit that you leave permanently connected to your computer, usually via a USB cable. When you're ready to download pictures from your camera, you place the camera into the dock, press a button or two, and the dock and camera work together to automatically start the transfer process.

Figure 3-6 shows a Kodak version of the camera-and-dock set-up, which the company refers to as its EasyShare system. In addition to assisting you with image transfers, the Kodak dock serves as the camera's battery charger. It also provides features that facilitate printing and e-mailing pictures. The dock sells as a separate accessory for about $130.

Figure 3-6: Compatible with some Kodak digital cameras, this camera dock simplifies the process of transferring, printing, and e-mailing images.

Printer Primer

Taking your digital photos from camera or computer to paper involves several decisions, not the least of which is choosing the right printer for the job. This section helps you sort through the various issues involved in printing your pictures, discussing the pros and cons of different types of printers, as well as whether you want to handle the job yourself or have a commercial printer do the honours.

Printing your own

On the consumer front, several vendors, including Hewlett-Packard, Epson, Olympus, and Canon, sell printers that are specially designed for printing digital photos at home or in the office. Some of the newest printer models deliver prints that are indistinguishable from the best traditional film prints.

You'll encounter a few options when you go printer shopping. Each type of printer offers advantages and disadvantages, and the technology you choose depends on your budget, your printing needs, and your print-quality expectations. To help you make sense of things, the following sections discuss the main categories of consumer and small-office printers.

Inkjet printers

Inkjet printers work by forcing little drops of ink through nozzles onto the paper. Inkjet printers designed for the home office or small business start at around $100 and can run several hundred dollars more. Higher-priced inkjets offer speedier printing and extra features, such as the ability to output on wider paper, produce borderless prints, hook up to a network, or print directly from a camera memory card.

Most inkjet printers enable you to print on plain paper or thicker (and more expensive) photographic stock, either with a glossy or matte finish. That flexibility is great because you can print rough drafts and everyday work on plain paper and save the more costly photographic stock for final prints and important projects.

Inkjets fall into two basic categories:

- ✔ General-purpose models, which are engineered to do a decent job on both text and pictures
- ✔ Photo printers, sometimes called *photocentric* printers, which are geared solely toward printing images. Photo-centric printers produce better-quality photos than all-purpose printers, but they're typically not well suited to everyday text printing because the print speed is slower than on a general-purpose machine.

That's not to say that you should expect lightning-fast prints from a general-purpose inkjet, though. Even on the fastest inkjet, outputting a colour image can take several minutes if you use the highest-quality print settings. And with some printers, you can't perform any other functions on your printer until the print job is complete.

In addition, the wet ink can cause the paper to warp slightly, and the ink can smear easily until the print dries. You can lessen both of these effects by using specially coated inkjet paper.

Despite these flaws, inkjets remain a good, economical solution for many users. Newer inkjet models incorporate refined technology that produces much higher image quality, less colour bleeding, and less page warping than models in years past.

Laser printers

Laser printers use a technology similar to that used in photo-copiers. I doubt that you want to know the details, so let me just say that the process involves a laser beam, which produces electric charges on a drum, which rolls toner — the ink, if you will — onto the paper. Heat is applied to the page to permanently affix the toner to the page (which is why pages come out of a laser printer warm).

Colour lasers can produce near-photographic quality images as well as excellent text. They're faster than inkjets, and you don't need to use any special paper (although you get better results if you use a high-grade laser paper as opposed to cheap copier paper).

The downside to colour lasers? Price. Although they've become much more affordable over the past two years, colour lasers still run $1,500 and up. And these printers tend to be big in stature as well as price — this isn't a machine that you want to use in a small home office that's tucked into a corner of your kitchen.

However, if you have the need for high-volume colour output, a colour laser printer can make sense. Although you pay more up front than you do for an inkjet, you should save money over time because the price of *consumables* (toner or ink, plus paper) is usually lower for laser printing than inkjet printing. Many colour lasers also offer networked printing, making them attractive to offices where several people share the same printer.

Dye-sub (thermal dye) printers

Dye-sub is short for *dye-sublimation,* which is worth remembering only for the purpose of one-upping the former science-fair winner who lives down the street. Dye-sub printers (also called *thermal-dye* printers) transfer images to paper using a plastic film or ribbon that's coated with coloured dyes. During the printing process, heating elements move across the film, causing the dye to fuse to the paper.

Like the newest photocentric inkjet printers, dye-sub printers deliver very good photo quality. Dye-sub printers manufactured for the consumer market fall within the same price range as quality photocentric inkjets, but they present a few disadvantages that may make them less appropriate for your home or office than an inkjet.

First, most dye-sub printers can output only snapshot size prints, although a few new models can produce 7.5 x 10-inch prints. More important, you have to use special stock that works expressly with dye-sub printers. That means that dye-sub printing isn't appropriate for general-purpose documents; these machines are purely photographic tools. The cost per print depends on the size of the paper.

How long will your prints last?

In addition to the issues presented in the preceding discussion of printer types, another important factor to consider when deciding on a printer is print stability — that is, how long you can expect the prints to last.

All photographs are subject to fading and colour shifts over time. Researchers say that a standard film print has a life expectancy of anywhere from 10 to 60 years, depending on the photographic paper, the printing process, and exposure to ultraviolet light and airborne pollutants, such as ozone. Those same criteria affect the stability of photos that you output on your home or office printer.

Unfortunately, the technologies capable of delivering image quality equal to a traditional photograph — dye-sub and inkjet printing — produce prints that can degrade rapidly, especially when displayed in bright light. Hang a print in front of a sunny window, and you may notice fading or colour change in as little as a few months.

Manufacturers have been scrambling to address this issue, and several possible solutions have been introduced that promise a longer print life expectancy when special inks and papers are used. However, because of the special archival inks, the *colour gamut* — range of colours — that these printers can reproduce is smaller than with standard inkjets.

The truth is, though, that no one really knows just how long a print from any of these new printers — inkjet or dye-sub — will last because they just haven't been around that long. The estimates given by manufacturers are based on lab tests that try to simulate the effect of years of exposure to light and atmospheric contaminants. But the research results are pretty varied, and the anticipated photo life you can expect from any printing system depends on whose numbers you use.

Also keep in mind that you can always take important images to a photo lab for output on archival photographic paper. For more information, see "Letting the pros do it," later in this chapter. Also see the upcoming sidebar, "Protecting your prints," for tips on making your prints last as long as possible.

Protecting your prints

No matter what the type of print, you can help keep its colours bright and true by adhering to the following storage and display guidelines:

✔ If you're having the picture framed, always mount the photo behind a matte to prevent the print from touching the glass. Be sure to use acid-free, archival matte board and UV-protective glass.

✔ Display the picture in a location where it isn't exposed to strong sunlight or fluorescent light for long periods of time.

✔ In photo albums, slip pictures inside acid-free, archival sleeves.

✔ Don't adhere prints to a matte board or other surface using masking tape, scotch tape, or other household products. Instead, use acid-free mounting materials, sold in art-supply stores and some craft stores.

✔ Limit exposure to humidity, wide temperature swings, cigarette smoke, and other airborne pollutants, as these can also contribute to image degradation.

✔ For the ultimate protection, always keep a copy of the image file on a CD-ROM or other storage medium so that you can output a new print if the original one deteriorates.

Letting the pros do it

Churning out photographic-quality prints of your digital images can be a pricey proposition. When you consider the cost of special photographic paper along with special inks or coatings that your printer may require, you can easily spend well over $1 for each print. In addition, unless you use archival papers and inks, your prints may not retain their original beauty as long as a traditional print.

When you want high-quality, long-lasting prints, you may find it easier and even more economical to let the professional printers handle your output needs. Here are a few options to consider:

✔ For top-notch photographic prints, try a commercial imaging lab that's geared to serving the needs of professional photographers and graphic artists. Such labs now offer printing of digital files on archival photographic paper. You can output a proof copy of your image on your home or office printer, and the lab can match the colours in your final print to that proof. Prices will vary depending on area, and the price per print typically goes down if you buy multiple copies of the same picture. Be sure to ask the lab to explain the different printing and paper options as well as how to prepare and submit your files.

✔ Web-based print services offer an option to photographers without access to a walk-in lab. You transmit your images to the company over the Internet and receive your printed images in the mail. One online lab to try is the Black's Online PhotoCentre (www.blackphoto.com).

✔ If you need more than 50 copies of an image or you want to print on a special stock — for example, a coloured stock — call upon the services of a commercial printer or service bureau. You can then have your images reproduced using traditional four-colour CMYK printing. The cost per printed image will depend on the number of images you need (typically, the more you print, the lower the per-print cost) and the type of stock you use.

Long-Term Picture Storage Options

In the professional digital imaging world, the hot new topic is *digital asset management.* Digital asset management — which, incredibly, is often referred to by its initials — simply refers to the storing and cataloguing of image files. Professional graphic artists and digital photographers accumulate huge collections of images and are always striving for better ways to save and inventory their assets.

Your image collection may not be as large as that of a professional photographer's, but at some point, you, too, need to think about where to keep all those photos you take. You may be at that point now if you shoot high-resolution pictures and your computer's hard drive is already cramped for space.

Additional storage options are plentiful — provided you have the cash, you can add as many digital closets and shoe boxes to your system as you want. For starters, you can add an additional hard drive to your computer. Several companies, including Maxtor, offer external hard drives geared specifically to people who need to store large picture and media files. You can buy a 40GB external Maxtor drive for about $200.

 Although adding a second hard drive may temporarily solve your picture storage concerns, you may also want to invest in a storage device that copies data to removable media. Because hard drives do fail on occasion, making backup copies on removable media is a good idea for special pictures. In addition, this option enables you to give copies of your picture files to other people, something you can't do if you have only a hard drive for image storage. If you do purchase a removable media storage device, you may be able to do without additional hard drive space.

The following list looks at a few of the most popular removable media devices for home and small-office users. Chapter 6 introduces you to some cataloguing programs that can help you keep track of all your images after you stow them away.

✔ The most common removable storage option is the floppy disk. Almost every computer today, with the exception of the iMac and iBook from Apple, has a floppy disk drive. The disks themselves are incredibly cheap: You can get a floppy for less than $1 if you watch the sale ads. The problem is that a floppy disk holds less than 1.5MB of data, which means that it's suitable for storing small, low-resolution, or highly compressed images, but not large, high-resolution, uncompressed pictures.

✔ Several companies offer removable storage devices commonly known as *super floppies.* These drives save data on disks that are just a little larger than a floppy but hold much more data. The most popular option is the Iomega Zip drive, available in 100MB and 250MB versions. Many vendors now include Zip drives as standard equipment on desktop and even laptop computers. Adding a Zip drive to your system runs about $150 for the smaller-capacity drive and $225 for the 250MB drive. A 100MB disk costs around $15; a 250MB disk sets you back about $25.

✔ Perhaps the most affordable and convenient option for long-term storage is a CD recorder, which tech-heads refer to as a *CD burner.* Several manufacturers now make CD recorders aimed at the consumer and small-business market. Figure 3-7 shows an external Hewlett-Packard CD model. You can pick up a CD recorder for under $150, and the CDs themselves, which can store as much as 650MB of data, cost from $.50 to $3, depending on which type you buy. (See the upcoming sidebar "CD-R or CD-RW?" for more on different types of CDs and CD recorders.)

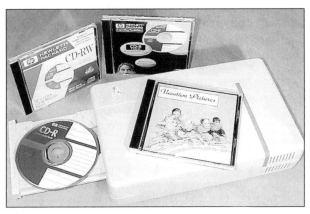

Figure 3-7: Burning your own CDs offers an inexpensive means of storing and sharing digital photos.

Recording your own CDs is by no means as carefree a prospect as copying files to a floppy disk or Zip disk. First, some compatibility issues exist that make it impossible for some types of homemade CDs to be read by some older computers. Second, even with software wizards to guide you, you still must deal with plenty of new and confusing technical terminology when choosing recording options. So if techno-babble intimidates you and the occasional unexplained glitch tempts you to put your fist through your computer monitor, you may want to hold off on a CD recorder. Or at the very least, ask your neighbourhood computer guru to help you install and set up the recorder.

✔ A close cousin to the CD burner, DVD-R and DVD-RW writers enable you to record your photos onto a DVD (digital video disc). What's the difference between CDs and DVDs? Capacity, mostly. A single DVD stores 4.7GB of data, while a CD holds about 650MB.

Although DVD is poised to overtake the CD as the most popular archival storage option in the next few years, it's too expensive and new for me to recommend it as a solution for the average photographer just yet. Stand-alone DVD burners cost about $500–600, although some computer makers do offer built-in DVD recorders as standard equipment on high-end models. More important, the industry doesn't seem to have settled firmly on a DVD format, which means that DVDs that you burn today may not be readable by tomorrow's DVD players. And of course, you can't share a DVD with people whose computers have only the more common CD-ROM drive.

As with any computer data, digital-image data will degrade over time. How soon you begin to lose data depends on the storage media you choose. With devices that use magnetic media, which includes hard drives, Zip disks and floppies, image deterioration starts to become noticeable after about ten years. In other words, don't rely on magnetic media for long-term archiving of images.

To give your images the longest possible life, opt for CD-ROM storage, which gives you about 100 years before data loss becomes noticeable. However, to get this storage life, you need to select the right type of CD media. If you're having your images transferred to CD at a professional lab, request archival-quality CDs; if you're burning your own CDs, use CD-R, not CD-RW,

CD-R or CD-RW?

CD recorders enable you to *burn* your own CDs — that is, copy image files or other data onto a compact disc (CD). Two types of CD recording exist: CD-R and CD-RW. The *R* stands for *recordable; RW* stands for *rewriteable.*

With CD-R, you can record data until the disc is full. But you can't delete files to make room for new ones — after you fill the disc once, you're done. On the plus side, your images can never be accidentally erased. Additionally, CD-R discs have a life expectancy of approximately 100 years, making them ideal for long-term archiving of important images. CD-R discs are cheap, too, selling for about $.50 each or even less if you happen upon a special store promotion. (However, because quality can vary from brand to brand, I recommend that you stay away from no-name, ultra-cheap CD-R discs and stick with high-quality discs from a respected manufacturer for your important image archives.)

With CD-RW, your CD works just like any other storage medium. You can get rid of files you no longer want and store new files in their place. Although CD-RW discs cost more than CD-R discs — about $2 each — they can be less expensive over the long run because you can reuse them as you do a floppy disk or Zip disk. For a couple of reasons, however, you shouldn't rely on CD-RW discs for archiving: You can accidentally over-write or erase an important image file, and data on CD-RW discs starts to degrade after about 30 years.

One other important factor distinguishes CD-R from CD-RW: compatibility with existing CD-ROM drives. If you're creating CDs to share images with other people, you should know that those people need *multiread* CD drives to access files on a CD-RW disc. This type of CD drive is being implemented in many new computer systems, but most older systems do not have multiread drives. Older computers can usually read CD-R discs without problems, however. (Depending on the recording software you use, you may need to format and record the disc using special options that ensure compatibility with older CD drives.)

Industry experts predict that CD-RW devices will soon be standard equipment in all new computer systems, so more people will be able to access CD-RW discs. For now, if you're shopping for a CD recorder, be aware that some recorders can write to CD-R discs only, while other recorders can write to both CD-R and CD-RW discs. The best bet is a machine that gives you the option of creating either CD-R or CD-RW discs. You can use the cheaper and more widely supported CD-R discs for archiving images and distributing your photos to others and use CD-RW discs for routine storage.

discs in your CD recorder. CD-RW discs have an estimated
life of just 30 years. (See the sidebar "CD-R or CD-RW?" for
information on the difference between CD-R and CD-RW discs.)

When choosing a storage option, also remember that the
various types of disks aren't interchangeable. Floppy disks, for
example, don't fit in a Zip drive. So if you want to be able to
swap images regularly with friends, relatives, or co-workers,
you need a storage option that's in widespread use. You
probably know many people who have a CD-ROM drive, for
example, but you may not find anybody in your circle of
acquaintances using a Zip drive. Also, if you're going to send
images to a service bureau or commercial printer on a regular
basis, find out what types of media it accepts before making
your purchase.

Software Solutions

Flashy and sleek, digital cameras are the natural stars of the
digital-imaging world. But without the software that enables
you to access and manipulate your images, your digital camera
would be nothing more than an overpriced paperweight.
Because I know that you have plenty of other had-to-have-it,
never-use-it devices that can serve as paperweights, the
following sections introduce you to some software products
that help you get the most from your digital camera.

Image-editing software

Image-editing software enables you to alter your digital photos
in just about any way you see fit. You can correct problems
with brightness, contrast, colour balance, and the like. You can
crop out excess background and get rid of unwanted image
elements. You can also apply special effects, combine pictures
into a collage, and explore countless other artistic notions.
Part IV of this book offers a brief introduction to photo editing
to get you started.

Today's computer stores, mail-order catalogues, and online
shopping sites are stocked with an enormous array of photo-
editing products. But all these programs can be loosely
grouped into two categories: entry-level and advanced. The
following sections help you determine which type of software
fits your needs best.

Entry-level photo-editing programs

Several companies offer programs geared to the photo-editing novice; popular choices include Ulead PhotoExpress, Jasc After Shot, and Microsoft Picture It!, all available for about $50.

All of these programs provide a basic set of image-correction tools plus plenty of on-screen handholding. *Wizards* (step-by-step on-screen guides) walk you through different editing tasks, and project templates simplify the process of adding your photo to a business card, calendar, e-mail postcard, or greeting card.

Within this category, the range of editing and effects tools provided varies widely, so you should read product reviews before buying to make sure that the program you get will enable you to do the photographic projects you have in mind.

Advanced photo-editing programs

Although the entry-level programs discussed in the preceding section provide enough tools to keep most casual users happy, people who edit pictures on a daily basis or just want a little more control over their images may want to move up the software ladder a notch. Ranging in price from $100 to $700, advanced photo-editing programs provide you with more flexible, more powerful, and, often, more convenient image-editing tools than entry-level offerings.

What kind of additional features do you get for your money? Here's just one example to illustrate the differences between beginner and advanced programs. Say that you want to retouch an image that's overexposed. In an entry-level program, you typically are limited to adjusting the exposure for all colours in the image by the same degree. But in an advanced program, you can adjust the highlights, shadows, and midtones (areas of medium brightness) independently — so you can make a businessman's white shirt even whiter without also giving his dark brown hair and beige suit a bleach job.

Additionally, using tools known as *dodge* and *burn tools,* you can "brush on" lightness and darkness as if you were painting with a paintbrush. In some programs, you can apply exposure adjustments in a way that preserves all the original image data in case you decide later that you don't like the results of your changes. And that's but a sampling of your many options — all just for adjusting exposure.

Advanced programs also include tools that enable power-users to accomplish complicated tasks more quickly. Some programs enable you to record a series of editing steps and then play the editing routine back to apply those same edits to a batch of images, for example.

The downside to advanced programs is that they can be intimidating to new users and also require a high learning curve. You usually don't get much on-screen assistance or any of the templates and wizards provided in beginner-level programs. Expect to spend plenty of time with the program manual or a third-party book to become proficient at using the software tools.

Price is also a drawback, especially if you opt for the premium player in the advanced category, Adobe Photoshop (about $1,000), geared to the professional photographer and digital artist. Fortunately, several good, less-expensive alternatives exist for users who don't need every possible bell and whistle. For under $150, Jasc Paint Shop Pro and Ulead PhotoImpact are two to consider. Another good choice in the same price range is Adobe Photoshop Elements (about $150), which includes Photoshop's basic power tools but also provides some of the same types of help features provided in consumer-level programs.

Before you invest in any imaging program, no matter how expensive, you're smart to give the program a whirl on your computer, using your images. You can find demo and trial versions of several image-editing programs at the Web sites of the software vendors.

Specialty software

In addition to programs designed specifically for photo editing, you can find some great niche programs geared to special digital photography needs and interests. The following list discusses some of the best programs I've found:

> ✔ Programs that I call *photo-utility* software are designed for digital photographers who simply need a quick way to print their images or send them with an e-mail message. Print Station, for example, simplifies the process of printing multiple images on the same sheet of paper.

✔ Image-cataloguing programs assist you in keeping track of all your images. As mentioned earlier in this chapter, some industry gurus refer to these programs as digital asset management (DAM) tools. But you can just call them cataloguing programs and get along fine with me. I don't think you want to walk into a computer store and ask to see all the DAM programs, anyway. At any rate, Chapter 6 provides more information about this kind of software.

✔ Image-stitching programs enable you to combine a series of images into a panoramic photo — similar to the kind you can take with some point-and-shoot film cameras. Chapter 5 offers more information on the concept.

✔ Finally, you can find several programs that fall into the "pure fun" category, such as BrainsBreaker, shown in Figure 3-8. With this $20 program, you can turn any photo into a digital jigsaw puzzle. You put the puzzle together by dragging pieces into place with your mouse — an endeavour that I find enormously addictive, I should add.

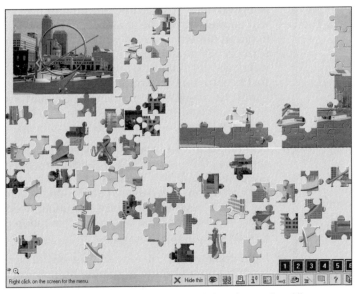

Figure 3-8: BrainsBreaker turns any digital photo into a virtual jigsaw puzzle.

Camera Accessories

So far, this chapter has focused on accessories to make your life easier and more fun after you shoot your digital pictures. But the items in the following list are even more essential because they help you capture great pictures in the first place:

- **Special lens adapter and lenses:** If your camera can accept other lenses, you can expand your range of creativity by investing in a wide-angle, close-up, or telephoto lens (telephoto lenses are designed for making faraway objects appear closer). With some cameras, you can add supplementary wide-angle and telephoto elements that slip over the normal camera lens. The price range of these accessories varies depending on the quality and type and whether or not you need a separate adapter to fit the lens to your camera.

- **Tripod:** If your pictures continually suffer from soft focus, camera shake is one possible cause — and using a tripod is a good cure. You can spend a little or a lot on a tripod, with models available for anywhere from $20 to several hundred dollars. I can tell you that I've been quite happy with my $20 model, though. And at that price, I don't worry about tossing the thing into the trunk when I travel. Just be sure that the tripod you buy is sturdy enough to handle the weight of your camera. You may want to take your camera with you when you shop so that you can see how well the tripod works with your camera.

- **LCD hoods:** If you have difficulty viewing images on your camera's LCD monitor in bright light, you may want to invest in an LCD hood. Hoods wrap around the monitor to create a four-sided awning that reduces glare on the screen. Several companies, including Hoodman (www.hoodmanusa.com), make custom-tailored hoods for a variety of digital cameras.

- **Light dome or box:** If you use your digital camera to take product shots of shiny or sparkly objects, such as glass or jewellery, you may find it almost impossible to avoid getting reflections or glare from your flash or other light source. You can solve this problem by using a light dome or tent, which serves as a diffusion screen between the objects and the light source.

✔ **Camera case:** Digital cameras are sensitive pieces of electronic equipment, and if you want them to perform well, you need to protect them from hazards of daily life. No camera is likely to take great pictures after being dropped on the sidewalk, being banged around inside a briefcase, or suffering other physical abuse on a regular basis. So whenever you're not using the camera, you should stow it in a well-padded camera case.

At any camera store, you can buy a full-fledged digital camera bag that has room for your batteries and other gear. Some digital cameras do come with their own cases, but most of these cases are pretty flimsy and not up to the job of keeping your camera safe from harm. You're spending several hundred dollars on a camera, so do yourself a favour and invest a little more on a proper protective case.

Part II
Ready, Set, Shoot!

The 5ᵗʰ Wave   By Rich Tennant

In this part...

Digital cameras for the consumer market are categorized as "point-and-shoot" cameras. That is, you're supposed to be able to simply point the camera at your subject and shoot the picture.

But as is the case with point-and-shoot film cameras, picture-taking with a digital camera isn't quite as automatic as the camera manufacturers would like you to believe. Before you aim that lens and press the shutter button, you need to consider quite a few factors if you want to come away with a good picture, as this part of the book reveals.

Chapter 4 tells you everything you need to know about composition, lighting, and focus — three primary components of a great photograph. Chapter 5 covers issues specific to digital photography, such as choosing the right capture resolution and shooting pictures that you want to place in a photo collage or stitch together into a panorama.

By abandoning the point-and-shoot approach and adopting the think-point-and-shoot strategies outlined in this part, you, too, can turn out impressive digital photographs. At the very least, you will no longer wind up with pictures in which the top of your subject's head is cut off or the focus is so far gone that people ask why you took pictures on such a foggy day.

Chapter 4

Take Your Best Shot

- -

In This Chapter

▶ Composing your image for maximum impact

▶ Shooting with and without a flash

▶ Adjusting exposure

▶ Compensating for backlighting

▶ Shooting reflective objects

▶ Bringing your subject into focus

- -

*A*fter you figure out the mechanics of your camera — how to load the batteries, how to turn on the LCD, and so on — taking a picture is a simple process. Just aim the camera and press the shutter button. Taking a *good* picture, however, isn't so easy. Sure, you can record an okay image of your subject without much effort. But if you want a crisp, well-exposed, dynamic image, you need to consider a few factors before you point and shoot.

This chapter explores three basic elements that go into a superior image: composition, lighting, and focus. By mulling over the concepts presented in this chapter, you can begin to evolve from so-so picture taker to creative, knock-their-socks-off photographer. Chapter 5 takes you one step further in your photographic development — sorry, bad pun — by exploring some issues specifically related to shooting with digital cameras.

Composition 101

Consider the image in Figure 4-1. As pictures go, it's not bad. The subject, a statue at the base of the Soldiers and Sailors Monument in Indianapolis, is interesting enough. But overall, the picture is . . . well, boring.

Figure 4-1: This image falls flat because of its uninspired framing and angle of view.

Now look at Figure 4-2, which shows two additional images of the same subject, but with more powerful results. What makes the difference? In a word, *composition*. Simply framing the statue differently, zooming in for a closer view, and changing the camera angle create more captivating images.

Not everyone agrees on the "best" ways to compose an image — art being in the eye of the beholder and all that. For every composition rule, you can find an incredible image that proves the exception. That said, the following list offers some suggestions that can help you create images that rise above the ho-hum mark on the visual interest meter:

> ✔ Remember the rule of thirds. For maximum impact, don't place your subject smack in the centre of the frame, as was done in Figure 4-1. Instead, mentally divide the image

area into thirds, as illustrated in Figure 4-3. Then position the main subject elements at spots where the dividing lines intersect.

Figure 4-2: Getting closer to the subject and shooting from less-obvious angles results in more interesting pictures.

Figure 4-3: One rule of composition is to divide the frame into thirds and position the main subject at one of the intersection points.

✔ To add life to your images, compose the scene so that the viewer's eye is naturally drawn from one edge of the frame to the other, as in Figure 4-4. The figure in the image, also part of the Soldiers and Sailors Monument, appears ready to fly off into the big, blue yonder. You can almost feel the breeze blowing the torch's flame and the figure's cape.

Figure 4-4: To add life to your pictures, frame the scene so that the eye is naturally drawn from one edge of the image to the other.

✔ Avoid the plant-on-the-head syndrome. In other words, watch out for distracting background elements.

✔ Shoot your subject from unexpected angles. Again, refer to Figure 4-1. This image accurately represents the statue. But the picture is hardly as captivating as the images in Figure 4-2, which show the same subject from more unusual angles.

✔ Here's a trick for shooting children: Photograph them while they're lying down on the floor and looking up at the camera, as in Figure 4-5. Maybe the children you photograph live in pristine surroundings, but in my family, rooms full of children are also full of toys, sippy cups, and other kid paraphernalia, which can make getting an uncluttered shot difficult. So I simply shove everything off of a small area of carpet and have the kids get down on the floor and pose.

Figure 4-5: If you can't photograph kids without getting playroom clutter in the scene, have them lie down on an empty swatch of carpet.

✔ Another good approach for shooting the wee ones is to hunker down so that you can shoot at eye level. If your knees are as bad as mine, this tactic isn't as easy as it sounds — the getting-down-to-eye-level part is easy enough, but the getting-back-up isn't! But the results are worth the effort and resulting ice pack.

✔ Get close to your subject. Often, the most interesting shot is the one that reveals the small details, such as the laugh lines in a grandfather's face or the raindrop on the rose petal. Don't be afraid to fill the frame with your subject, either. The old rule about "head room" — providing a nice margin of space above and to the sides of a subject's head — is a rule meant to be broken on occasion.

✔ Try to capture the subject's personality. The most boring people shots are those in which the subjects stand in front of the camera and say "cheese" on the photographer's cue. If you really want to reveal something about your subjects, catch them in the act of enjoying a favourite hobby or using the tools of their trade. This tactic is especially helpful with subjects who are camera-shy; focusing their attention on a familiar activity helps put them at ease and replace that stiff, I'd-rather-be-anywhere-but-here look with a more natural expression.

A Parallax! A Parallax!

You compose your photo perfectly. The light is fine, the focus is fine, and all other photographic planets appear to be in alignment. But after you snap your picture and view the image on the camera monitor, the framing is off, as though your subject repositioned itself while you weren't looking.

You're not the victim of some cruel digital hoax — just a photographic phenomenon known as a *parallax error.*

On most digital cameras, as on most point-and-shoot film cameras, the viewfinder looks out on the world through a separate window from the camera lens. Because the viewfinder is located an inch or so above or to the side of the lens, it sees your subject from a slightly different angle than the lens. But the image is captured from the point of view of the lens, not the viewfinder.

When you look through your viewfinder, you should see some lines near the corners of the frame. The lines indicate the boundaries of the frame as seen by the camera lens. Pay attention to these framing cues, or you may wind up with pictures that appear to have been lopped off along one edge, as in Figure 4-6.

The closer you are to your subject, the bigger the parallax problem becomes, whether you use a zoom lens or simply position the camera lens nearer to your subject. Some cameras provide a second set of framing marks in the viewfinder to indicate the framing boundaries that apply when you're shooting close-up shots. Check your camera manual to determine which framing marks mean what. (Some markings have to do with focusing, not framing.)

Figure 4-6: My pal Bernie loses his ears as the result of a parallax error.

If your camera has an LCD monitor, you have an additional aid for avoiding parallax problems. Because the monitor reflects the image as seen by the lens, you can simply use the monitor instead of the viewfinder to frame your image. On some cameras, the LCD monitor turns on automatically when you switch to macro mode for close-up shooting.

Let There Be Light

Digital cameras are extremely demanding when it comes to light. A typical digital camera has a light sensitivity equivalent to that of ISO 100 film. (ISO film ratings and their implications are discussed in Chapter 2.) As a result, image detail tends to get lost when objects are in the shadows. Too much light can also create problems. A ray of sunshine bouncing off a highly reflective surface can cause *blown highlights* — areas where all image detail is lost, resulting in a big white blob in your picture.

Capturing just the right amount of light involves not only deciding whether to use a flash or external photographic lights, but also figuring out the right exposure settings. The following sections address everything you need to know to capture a well-lit, properly exposed image.

Keep in mind that you can correct minor lighting and exposure problems in the image-editing stage. Generally speaking, making a too-dark image brighter is easier than correcting an overexposed (too bright) image. So if you can't seem to get the exposure just right, opt for a slightly underexposed image rather than an overexposed one.

Locking in (auto) exposure

Exposure refers to the amount of light captured by the camera. (Read Chapter 2 for a complete discussion of exposure.) Most consumer-level digital cameras feature *autoexposure,* sometimes known as *programmed autoexposure,* in which the camera reads the amount of light in the scene and then sets the exposure automatically for you.

In order for your camera's autoexposure mechanism to work correctly, you need to take this three-step approach to shooting your pictures:

1. **Frame your subject.**

2. **Press the shutter button halfway down and hold it there.**

   The camera analyzes the scene and sets the focus and exposure. (Upcoming sections discuss the focus side of the equation.) After the camera makes its decisions, it signals you in some fashion — usually with a blinking light near the viewfinder or with a beeping noise.

   If you don't want your subject to appear in the middle of the frame, you can recompose the image after locking in the exposure and focus. Just keep holding the shutter button halfway down as you reframe the image in your viewfinder. Don't move or reposition the subject before you shoot, or the exposure and focus may be out of whack.

3. **Press the shutter button the rest of the way down to take the picture.**

On lower-end cameras, you typically get a choice of two autoexposure settings — one appropriate for shooting in very bright light and another for average lighting. Many cameras display a warning light or refuse to capture the image if you've chosen an autoexposure setting that will result in a badly overexposed or underexposed picture. Higher-priced cameras give you more control over autoexposure, as discussed in the next few sections.

Choosing a metering mode

Some higher-priced digital cameras enable you to choose from several *metering modes.* (Check your manual to find out what buttons or menu commands to use to access the different modes.) In plain English, *metering mode* refers to the way in which the camera's autoexposure mechanism meters — measures — the light in the scene while calculating the proper exposure for your photograph. The typical options are as follows:

✔ **Matrix metering:** Sometimes known as *multizone metering,* this mode divides the frame into a grid (matrix) and analyzes the light at many different points on the grid. The camera then chooses an exposure that best captures both shadowed and brightly lit portions of the scene. This mode is typically the default setting and works well in most situations.

✔ **Centre-weighted metering:** When set to this mode, the camera measures the light in the entire frame but assigns a greater importance — weight — to the centre quarter of the frame. Use this mode when you're more concerned about how stuff in the centre of your picture looks than stuff around the edges. (How's that for technical advice?)

✔ **Spot metering:** In this mode, the camera measures the light only at the centre of the frame. Spot metering is helpful when the background is much brighter than the subject — for example, when you're shooting backlit scenes (subjects that are in front of the sun or another light source). In matrix or centre-weighted metering mode, your subject may be underexposed because the camera reduces the exposure to account for the brightness of the background.

When using spot-metering mode, compose your image so that your main subject is in the centre of the frame and lock in the exposure and focus as explained in "Locking in (auto) exposure," earlier in this chapter. See the section "Compensating for backlighting," later in this chapter, for other tricks for dealing with this shooting scenario.

Adjusting ISO

As you know if you explored Chapter 2, film is assigned an ISO number to indicate light sensitivity. The higher the number, the "faster" the film — meaning that it reacts more quickly to light, enabling you to shoot in dim lighting without a flash or to use a faster shutter speed or smaller aperture.

Some digital cameras also offer a choice of ISO settings, which theoretically gives you the same flexibility as working with different speeds of film. I say "theoretically" because raising the ISO has a downside that usually outweighs the potential advantage.

Pictures shot at a higher ISO tend to suffer from *noise,* which is a fancy way of referring to a speckled, grainy texture. Faster film also produces grainier pictures than slower film, but the quality difference seems to be greater when you shoot digitally. When you print pictures at a small size, the texture produced by the excess grain may not be apparent to the eye; instead, the image may have a slightly blurry look.

For some shooting scenarios, you may be forced to use a higher ISO if you want to get the picture. And if you're trying to capture a moving subject, you may need to raise the ISO in order to use the fast shutter speed necessary to freeze the action.

The bottom line is this: Experiment with ISO settings if your camera offers them, and by all means, go with a higher ISO if the alternative is not getting the shot at all. But for best picture quality, keep the ISO at its lowest or next-to-lowest setting. (How far up you can go depends on the camera, so take some test shots to evaluate quality at each setting.)

Applying exposure compensation

Exposure compensation, also referred to as EV (*exposure value*) adjustment, bumps the exposure up or down a few notches from what the camera delivers at the autoexposure setting.

How you get to the exposure compensation settings varies from camera to camera. But you typically choose from settings such as +0.7, +0.3, 0.0, –0.3, –0.7, and so on, with the 0.0 representing the default autoexposure setting.

A positive EV value increases the exposure, resulting in a brighter image. To decrease the exposure, choose a negative EV value.

Different cameras provide you with different ranges of exposure options, and the extent to which an increase or decrease in the exposure value affects your image also varies from camera to camera.

Figure 4-7 shows how a few exposure settings available on a Nikon digital camera affected a picture that I shot indoors, without a flash. The middle image shows the exposure that the camera created when I set the EV value to 0.0. The left image shows the same shot when I reduced the exposure by using a negative EV value (–1.0); the right image shows what happened when I increased the exposure by using a positive EV value (+1.0).

EV -1.0   EV 0.0   EV +1.0

Figure 4-7: By raising or lowering the EV value, you can adjust the autoexposure mechanism to produce a lighter or darker image.

Figure 4-7 points up the benefits of exposure compensation. I wanted an exposure that was dark enough to allow the candle flame to create a soft glow and capture the contrast between the shadowed background areas and the bands of strong afternoon sunshine, which were coming in through the slats of a wooden blind. The non-adjusted exposure (labeled 0.0) was just a bit brighter than I had in mind. So I just played with the

EV values until I came up with a mix of shadows and highlights that suited the subject, which, for my purposes, was the result I obtained with an EV setting of –0.3.

Don't forget that if your camera offers a choice of metering modes, you may want to experiment with changing the metering mode as well as using EV adjustment. Adjusting the metering mode changes the area of the frame that the camera considers when making its exposure decision. In the candle image, I used matrix-metering mode.

Using aperture- or shutter-priority mode

Cameras at the higher end of the consumer-model price tier enable you to switch from regular autoexposure mode, where the camera sets both aperture and shutter speed, to *aperture-priority* autoexposure or *shutter-priority* autoexposure. These options work as follows:

✔ **Aperture-priority autoexposure:** This mode gives you control over the aperture. After setting the aperture, you frame your shot and then press the shutter button halfway down to set the focus and exposure, as you do when using programmed autoexposure mode. But this time, the camera checks to see what aperture you chose and then selects the shutter speed necessary to correctly expose the image at that aperture.

By altering the aperture, you can control depth of field — the range of sharp focus.

✔ **Shutter-priority autoexposure:** If you work in shutter-priority mode, you choose the shutter speed, and the camera selects the correct aperture. (If you're not sure what the terms *shutter speed* and *aperture* mean, check out Chapter 2.)

Theoretically, you should wind up with the same exposure no matter what aperture or shutter speed you choose, because as you adjust one value, the camera makes a corresponding change to the other value, right? Well, yes, sort of. Keep in mind that you're working with a limited range of shutter speeds and apertures (your camera manual provides information on available settings). So depending on the lighting conditions, the camera may not be able to properly compensate for the shutter speed or aperture that you choose.

Suppose that you're shooting outside on a bright, sunny day. You shoot your first picture at an aperture of f/11, and the picture looks great. Then you shoot a second picture, this time choosing an aperture of f/4. The camera may not be able to set the shutter speed high enough to accommodate the larger aperture, which means an overexposed picture.

Here's another example of how things can go wrong: Say that you're trying to catch a tennis player in the act of smashing a ball over the net on a grey overcast day. You know that you need a high shutter speed to capture action, so you switch to shutter-priority mode and set the shutter speed to 1/300 second. But given the dim lighting, the camera can't capture enough light even at the largest aperture setting. So your picture turns out too dark.

As long as you keep the camera's shutter speed and aperture range in mind, however, switching to shutter-priority or aperture-priority mode can come in handy in the following scenarios:

- ✔ You can't get the camera to produce the exposure you want in programmed autoexposure mode or by playing with EV compensation adjustment (see the preceding section) or metering mode.

- ✔ You're trying to capture an action scene, and the shutter speed the camera selects in programmed autoexposure mode is too slow.

- ✔ You purposefully want to use a too-slow shutter speed so that your picture looks a little blurry, creating a sense of motion.

- ✔ You want to alter depth of field.

Adding a flash of light

If the techniques discussed in preceding sections don't deliver a bright enough exposure, you simply have to find a way to bring more light onto your subject. The obvious choice, of course, is to use a flash.

Most digital cameras, like point-and-shoot film cameras, have a built-in flash that operates in several modes. You typically can choose from these options:

- **Auto flash:** In this mode, which is usually the default setting, the camera gauges the available light and fires the flash if needed.

- **Fill flash:** This mode triggers the flash regardless of the light in the scene. Fill-flash mode is especially helpful for outdoor shots, such as the one in Figure 4-8. I shot the image on the left using the auto-flash mode. Because this picture was taken on a bright sunny day, the camera didn't see the need for a flash. But I did because the shadow from the hat obscured the subject's eyes. Turning on the fill-flash mode threw some additional light on her face, bringing her eyes into visible range.

Figure 4-8: An outdoor image shot without a flash (left) and with a flash (right).

- **No flash:** Choose this setting when you don't want to use the flash, no way, no how. With digital photography, you may find yourself using this mode more than you may expect. Especially when you're shooting highly reflective objects, such as glass, a flash can cause blown highlights. You usually get better results if you turn off the flash and use alternate light sources (as explained in the next section) or boost the exposure using your camera's exposure adjustments, if available. The upcoming section "Lighting shiny objects" offers more help with this problem.

You may also want to turn off the flash simply because the quality of the existing light is part of what makes the scene compelling. The interplay of shadows and light is the interesting aspect of the scene, which is another way of looking at the shadows cast in Figure 4-8.

When you turn off the flash, remember that the camera may reduce the shutter speed to compensate for the dim lighting. That means that you need to hold the camera steady for a longer period of time to avoid blurry images. Use a tripod or otherwise brace the camera for best results.

✓ **Flash with red-eye reduction:** Anyone who's taken people pictures with a point-and-shoot camera — digital or film — is familiar with the so-called red-eye problem. The flash reflects in the subject's eyes, and the result is a demonic red glint in the eye. Red-eye reduction mode aims to thwart this phenomenon by firing a low-power flash before the "real" flash goes off or by lighting a little lamp for a second or two prior to capturing the image. The idea is that the prelight, if you will, causes the iris of the eye to shut down a little, thereby lessening the chances of a reflection when the final flash goes off.

Unfortunately, red-eye reduction on digital cameras doesn't work much better than it does on film cameras. Often, you still wind up with fire in the eyes — hey, the manufacturer only promised to *reduce* red eye, not eliminate it, right? Worse, your subjects sometimes think the preflash or light is the real flash and start walking away just when the picture is actually being captured. So if you shoot with red-eye mode turned on, be sure to explain to your subjects what's going to happen.

The good news is that, because you're shooting digitally, you can edit out those red eyes in your image-editing software. Use the painting techniques that I discuss in Chapter 9 to make your red eyes blue (or black, grey, green, or brown, as the case may be).

✓ **Slow-sync flash:** A few higher-end cameras offer this variation on the auto-flash mode. Slow-sync flash increases the exposure time beyond what the camera normally sets for flash pictures. With a normal flash, your main subject may be illuminated by the flash, but background elements beyond the reach of the flash may be obscured by darkness. With slow-sync flash, the longer exposure time helps make those background elements brighter.

✓ **External flash:** Another high-end option enables you to use a separate flash unit with your digital camera, just as you can with a 35mm SLR and other high-end film cameras. In this mode, the camera's on-board flash is disabled, and you must set the correct exposure to work with your flash. This option is a great one for professional photographers and advanced photo hobbyists who have the expertise and equipment to use it; check your camera manual to find out what type of external flash works with your camera and how to connect the flash.

If your camera has a built-in flash but doesn't offer an accessory off-camera flash connection, you can get the benefits of an external flash by using so-called "slave" flash units. These small, self-contained, battery-operated flash units have built-in photo eyes that trigger the supplemental flash when the camera's flash goes off. If you're trying to photograph an event in a room that's dimly lit, you can put several slave units in different places. All the units will fire when you take a picture anywhere in the room.

Switching on additional light sources

Although your camera's flash offers one alternative for lighting your scene, flash photography isn't problem-free. When you're shooting your subject at close range, a flash can cause blown highlights or leave some portions of the image looking overexposed. A flash can also lead to red-eyed people, as discussed in the preceding section.

But it looked good in the LCD!

If your camera has an LCD monitor, you can get a good idea of whether your image is properly exposed by reviewing it in the monitor. But don't rely entirely on the monitor, because it doesn't provide an absolutely accurate rendition of your image. Your actual image may be brighter or darker than it appears on the monitor, especially if your camera enables you to adjust the brightness of the monitor display.

To make sure that you get at least one correctly exposed image, *bracket* your shots if your camera offers exposure-adjustment controls. Bracketing means to record the same scene at several different exposure settings. Some cameras even offer an automatic bracketing feature that records multiple images, each at a different exposure, with one press of the shutter button.

Some digital cameras can accept an auxiliary flash unit, which helps reduce blown highlights and red eye because you can move the flash farther away from the subject. But if your camera doesn't offer this option, you usually get better results if you turn off the flash and use another light source to illuminate the scene.

If you're a well-equipped film photographer and you have studio lights, go dig them up. Or you may want to invest in some inexpensive photoflood lights — these are the same kind of lights used with video camcorders and are sometimes called "hot" lights because they "burn" continuously.

But you really don't need to go out and spend a fortune on lighting equipment. If you get creative, you can probably figure out a lighting solution using stuff you already have around the house. For example, when shooting small objects, I sometimes clear off a shelf on the white bookcase in my office. A nearby window offers a perfect natural light source.

For shots where I need a little more space, I sometimes use the set-up shown in Figure 4-9. The white background is nothing more than a cardboard presentation easel purchased at an art and education supply store — teachers use these things to create classroom displays. I placed another white board on the table surface.

The easel and board brighten up the subject because they reflect light onto it. If I need still more light, I switch on a regular old desk lamp or a small clip-on shop light (the kind you buy in hardware stores). And if I want a coloured background instead of a white one, I clip a piece of coloured tissue paper, also bought at that education supply store, onto the easel. A solid-coloured tablecloth or even a bed sheet works just as well as a background drape.

Okay, so professional photographers and serious amateurs will no doubt have a good laugh at these cheap little set-ups. But I say, whatever works, works. Besides, you've already spent a good sum of money on your camera, so why not save a few bucks where you can?

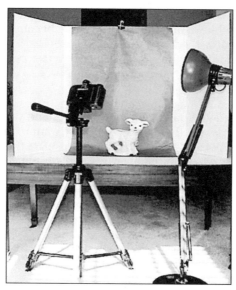

Figure 4-9: You can create a makeshift studio using nothing more than a sunny window, a white presentation easel, a tripod, and household lamp.

When using an artificial light source, whether it is a true-blue photography light or a makeshift solution like a desk lamp, you get better results if you don't aim the light directly at the object you're photographing. Instead, aim the light at the background and let the light bounce off that surface onto your subject. For example, when using a set-up like the one in Figure 4-9, you may aim the light at one of the side panels. This kind of lighting is called *bounce lighting,* in case you're curious.

Because different light sources have different *colour temperatures* (contain different amounts of red, green, and blue light), lighting a subject both with sunlight and an artificial light source, as shown in Figure 4-9, can confuse your camera. If your pictures exhibit an unwanted colour cast, try changing your camera's white-balance setting to fix the problem. Alternatively, you can buy some daylight photo flood bulbs to get the colour temperature of your artificial lights more in sync with the daylight shining through the window. For more details about white balance, check out Chapter 5.

Lighting shiny objects

When you shoot shiny objects such as jewellery, glass, chrome, and porcelain, lighting presents a real dilemma. Any light source that shines directly on the object can bounce off the surface and cause blown highlights, as shown in the left image in Figure 4-10. In addition, the light source or other objects in the room may be reflected in the surface of the object you want to shoot.

Figure 4-10: Shooting with a built-in flash creates blown highlights (left); abandoning the flash and working with a diffused light source solves the problem (right).

Professional photographers invest in expensive lighting set-ups and studio backdrops to avoid these problems when shooting product shots like the one in Figure 4-10. If you're not in the professional category — or just don't have a huge budget for outfitting a studio — try these tricks to get decent pictures of shiny stuff:

✔ First, turn off your camera's built-in flash and find another way to light the object. The built-in flash will create a strong, focused light source that's bound to create problems. See earlier sections in this chapter to find out how various digital camera features may enable you to get a good exposure without using a flash.

✔ Find a way to diffuse the lighting. Placing a white curtain or sheet between the light source and the object can not only soften the light and help prevent blown highlights, but also prevent unwanted reflections.

✔ If you regularly need to photograph small to medium-sized shiny objects, you may want to invest in a product like the Cloud Dome (visit www.clouddome.com). You put the objects you want to shoot under the dome and then attach your camera to a special mount, centring the camera lens over a hole in the top of the dome. The dome diffuses the light sources and eliminates reflections. In addition, the mount stabilizes the camera, eliminating camera shake that can cause a blurred image.

The Cloud Dome sells for around $300; less expensive models are available, as are extenders that allow for shooting taller or wider objects. The price may seem a little steep at first, but if you do a lot of this type of photography, the amount of time and frustration it can save may be well worth your investment.

Compensating for backlighting

A *backlit* picture is one in which the sun or light source is behind the subject. With autoexposure cameras, strong back-lighting often results in too-dark subjects because the camera sets the exposure based on the overall light in the scene, not just on the light on the subject. The left image in Figure 4-11 is a classic example of a backlighting problem.

To remedy the situation, you have several options:

✔ Reposition the subject so that the sun is behind the camera instead of behind the subject.

✔ Reposition yourself so that you're shooting from a different angle.

✔ Use a flash. Adding the flash can light up your subjects and bring them out of the shadows. However, because the working range of the flash on most consumer digital cameras is relatively small, your subject must be fairly close to the camera for the flash to do any good.

Figure 4-11: Backlighting can cause your subjects to appear lost in the shadows (left). Adjusting the exposure or using a flash can compensate for backlighting (right).

✔ If the backlighting isn't terribly strong and your camera offers exposure compensation, try raising the EV value, as explained in "Applying exposure compensation," earlier in this chapter. Check your camera's manual for information on using exposure compensation controls and other exposure options described elsewhere in this chapter.

Keep in mind that while increasing the exposure may brighten up your subjects, it may also cause the already bright portions of the scene to appear overexposed.

✔ If your camera offers a choice of metering modes, switch to spot metering or centre-weighted metering. Check out "Choosing a metering mode," earlier in this chapter, for information about metering modes.

✔ On cameras that don't offer spot or centre-weighted metering, meaning that the camera considers the light throughout the frame when setting the exposure, you can try to "fool" the autoexposure meter. Fill the frame with a dark object, press the shutter button halfway down to lock in the exposure, reframe the subject, and press the shutter button the rest of the way down to take the picture.

Because the focus is also set when you press the shutter button halfway, be sure that the dark object you're using to set the exposure is the same distance from the camera as your real subject. Otherwise, the focus of the picture will be off.

In the image on the right in Figure 4-11, I increased the exposure slightly and also used a flash. The image still isn't ideal — the subjects are still too dimly lit for my taste, and some regions border on being overexposed — but it's a vast improvement over the original. A little bit of additional brightness adjustment in a photo-editing program could improve things even more. To fix this image, I would raise the brightness level of the foreground subjects only, leaving the sky untouched. For information on this kind of image correction, see Chapter 8.

Excuse me, can you turn down the sun?

Adding more light to a scene is considerably easier than reducing the light. If you're shooting outdoors, you can't exactly hit the dimmer switch on the sun. If the light is too strong, you really have only a few options. You can move the subject into the shade (in which case you can use a fill flash to light the subject), or, on some cameras, reduce the exposure by lowering the EV value.

If you can't find a suitable shady backdrop, you can create one with a piece of cardboard. Just have a friend hold the cardboard between the sun and the subject. Voilà — instant shade. By moving the cardboard around, you can vary the amount of light that hits the subject.

Focus on Focus

Like point-and-shoot film cameras, digital cameras for the consumer market provide focusing aids to help you capture sharp images with ease. The following sections describe the different types of focusing schemes available and explain how to make the most of them.

Working with fixed-focus cameras

Fixed-focus cameras are just that — the focus is set at the factory and can't be changed. The camera is designed to capture sharply any subject within a certain distance from the lens. Subjects outside that range appear blurry.

Fixed-focus cameras sometimes are called *focus-free* cameras because you're free of the chore of setting the focus before you shoot. But this term is a misnomer, because even though you can't adjust the focus, you have to remember to keep the subject within the camera's focusing range. There is no such thing as a (focus) free lunch.

Be sure to check your camera manual to find out how much distance to put between your camera and your subject. With fixed-focus cameras, blurry images usually result from having your subject too close to the camera. (Most fixed-focus cameras are engineered to focus sharply from a few feet away from the camera to infinity.)

Taking advantage of autofocus

Most digital cameras offer autofocus, which means that the camera automatically adjusts the focus after measuring the distance between lens and subject. But "autofocusing" isn't totally automatic. For autofocus to work, you need to "lock in" the focus before you shoot the picture, as follows:

1. **Frame the picture.**

2. **Press the shutter button halfway down and hold it there.**

   Your camera analyzes the picture and sets the focus. If your camera offers autoexposure — as most do — the exposure is set at the same time. After the exposure and focus are locked in, the camera lets you know that you can proceed with the picture. Usually, a little light blinks near the viewfinder or the camera makes a beeping noise.

3. **Press the shutter button the rest of the way down to take the picture.**

Although autofocus is a great photography tool, you need to understand a few things about how your camera goes about its focusing work in order to take full advantage of this feature. Here's the condensed version of the autofocusing manual:

✔ Autofocus mechanisms fall into one of two main categories:

- **Single-spot focus:** With this type of autofocus, the camera reads the distance of the element that's at the centre of the frame in order to set the focus.

- **Multi-spot focus:** The camera measures the distance at several spots around the frame and sets focus relative to the nearest object.

You need to know how your camera adjusts focus so that when you lock in the focus (using the press-and-hold method just described), you place the subject within the area that the autofocus mechanism will read. If the camera uses single-spot focusing, for example, you should place your subject in the centre of the frame when locking the focus. Some cameras enable you to choose which type of focusing you want to use for a particular shot; check your camera manual for details.

✔ If your camera offers single-spot focus, you may see little framing marks in the viewfinder that indicate the focus point. Check your camera manual to see what the different viewfinder marks mean. On some cameras, the marks are provided to help you frame the picture rather than as a focusing indicator. (See the section "A Parallax! A Parallax!" earlier in this chapter for more information.)

✔ After you lock in the focus, you can reframe your picture if you want. As long as you keep the shutter button halfway down, the focus remains locked. Be careful that the distance between the camera and the subject doesn't change, or your focus will be off.

✔ Some cameras that offer autofocus also provide you with one or two manual-focus adjustments. Your camera may offer a *macro mode* for close-up shooting and an *infinity lock* or *landscape mode* for shooting subjects at a distance, for example. When you switch to these modes, auto-focusing may be turned off, so you need to make sure that your subject falls within the focusing range of the selected mode. Check your camera's manual to find out the proper camera-to-subject distance.

Focusing manually

On most consumer digital cameras, you get either no manual-focusing options or just one or two options in addition to autofocus. You may be able to choose a special focus setting for close-up shooting and one for faraway subjects.

But a few high-end cameras offer more extensive manual focusing controls. Although some models offer a traditional focusing mechanism where you twist the lens barrel to set the focus, most cameras require you to use menu controls to select the distance at which you want the camera to focus.

Hold that thing still!

A blurry image isn't always the result of poor focusing; you can also get fuzzy shots if you move the camera during the time the image is being captured.

Holding the camera still is essential in any shooting situation, but it becomes especially important when the light is dim because a longer exposure time is needed. That means that you have to keep the camera steady longer than you do when shooting in bright light.

To help keep the camera still, try these tricks:

✔ Press your elbows against your sides as you snap the picture.

✔ Squeeze, don't jab, the shutter button. Use a soft touch to minimize the chance of moving the camera when you press the shutter button.

✔ Place the camera on a countertop, table, or other still surface. Better yet, use a tripod. You can pick up an inexpensive tripod for about $20.

✔ If your camera offers a self-timer feature, you can opt for hands-free shooting to eliminate any possibility of camera shake. Place the camera on a tripod (or other still surface), set the camera to self-timer mode, and then press the shutter button (or do whatever your manual says to activate the self-timer mechanism). Then move away from the camera. After a few seconds, the camera snaps the picture for you automatically.

Of course, if you're lucky enough to own a camera that offers remote-control shooting, you can take advantage of that feature instead of the self-timer mode.

The ability to set the focus at a specific distance from the camera comes in handy when you want to shoot several pictures of one, stationary subject. By setting the focus manually, you don't have to go to the trouble of locking in the autofocus for each shot. Just be sure that you've accurately gauged the distance between camera and subject when setting the manual-focus distance.

If you're using manual focus for close-up shooting, get out a ruler and make sure that you have the correct camera-to-subject distance. You can't get a good idea of whether the focus is dead-on from the viewfinder or LCD, and being just an inch off in your focus judgment can mean a blurry picture.

Chapter 5

Digicam Dilemmas — and How to Solve Them

....

In This Chapter

▶ Choosing the right resolution and compression settings

▶ Getting your whites to be white

▶ Composing for digital creativity

▶ Devoting more pixels to your subject

▶ Working with optical and digital zoom

▶ Capturing action

▶ Shooting panoramas

▶ Avoiding grainy images

....

*M*ost of the tips and techniques in Chapter 4 apply not just to digital photography, but to film photography as well. This chapter is different.

Here, you find out how to tackle some of the challenges that are unique to digital photography. You also discover how to alter your shooting strategy to take advantage of the many new possibilities that are open to you now that you've gone digital.

In other words, it's time to look at photography from a pixel perspective.

Dialling In Your Capture Settings

Before you press the shutter button or even compose your image, you need to make a few decisions about how you want the camera to capture and store your images. Most digital cameras offer you a choice of image resolution and compression settings, and some cameras also enable you to store the image in one or two different file formats.

The following sections help you come to the right conclusions about your camera's resolution, compression, and file-format options.

Setting the capture resolution

Depending on your camera, you may be able to select from two or more image resolution settings. These settings determine how many horizontal and vertical pixels the image will contain, not pixels per inch (ppi). You set this second value in your photo editor before you print one of your digital pictures. (See Chapter 2 for the complete story on all this resolution stuff.)

On some cameras, resolution values are specified in pixels — 640 x 480, for example — with the horizontal pixel count always given first. But on other cameras, the different resolution settings go by such vague names as Basic, Fine, Superfine, and so on.

Your camera manual should spell out exactly how you go about changing the image resolution and how many pixels you get with each setting. You should also find information on how many images you can store per megabyte of camera memory at each setting.

When setting the camera resolution, consider the final output of the image. For Web or on-screen pictures, you can get by with 640 x 480 pixels or even 320 x 240 pixels. But if you want to print your picture, choose the capture setting that comes closest to giving you the output resolution — pixels per inch, or ppi — that your printer manual recommends.

For example, suppose that your camera offers the following resolution options: 640 x 480, 1024 x 768, and 1600 x 1200. Your printer manual tells you that the optimum output resolution for quality prints is 300 pixels per inch. If you capture the image at the lowest resolution, the print size at 300 ppi is around 2 inches wide by 1.6 inches tall. At 1024 x 768, you get a print size of about 3.4 x 2.5 inches; at 1600 x 1200, about 5 x 4. (These are just loose guidelines; you may be able to get good prints with fewer pixels per inch.)

 Of course, the more pixels, the bigger the picture file and the more memory your image consumes. So if your camera has limited memory and you're shooting at a location where you won't be able to download images, you may want to choose a lower resolution setting so that you can fit more pictures into the available memory. Alternatively, you can select a higher degree of image compression (discussed in the next section) to reduce file size.

 On some cameras, capture resolution is lowered automatically when you use certain features. For example, many cameras provide a burst mode that enables you to record a series of images with one press of the shutter button (see "Catching a Moving Target," later in this chapter). When you use this mode, most cameras reduce the capture resolution to 640 x 480 pixels or lower. Cameras that offer a choice of ISO settings also typically limit resolution at the highest settings. (Chapter 2 explains ISO.)

Choosing a compression setting

Your camera probably provides a control for choosing the amount of *compression* that is applied to your images. In short, compression trims some data out of an image file so that its file size is reduced.

 Lossless compression removes only redundant image data so that any change in image quality is virtually undetectable. But because lossless compression often doesn't result in a significant shrinking of file size, most digital cameras use *lossy compression,* which is less discriminating when dumping data. Lossy compression is great at reducing file size, but you pay the price in reduced image quality. The more compression you apply, the more your image suffers.

Typically, compression settings are given the same vague monikers as resolution settings: Good/Better/Best or High/Normal/Basic, for example. Remember that these names refer not to the type or amount of compression being applied, but to the resulting image quality. If you set your camera to the Best setting, for example, the image is less compressed than if you choose the Good setting. Of course, the less you compress the image, the larger its file size, and the fewer images you can fit in the available camera memory.

Because all cameras provide different compression options, you need to consult your manual to find out what the options on your particular model do. Typically, you find a chart in the manual that indicates how many images you can fit into a certain amount of memory at different compression settings. But you need to experiment to find out exactly how each setting affects picture quality. Shoot the same image at several different compression settings to get an idea of how much damage you do to your pictures if you opt for a higher degree of compression. If your camera offers several capture resolution settings, do the compression test for each resolution setting.

As you choose your capture settings, remember that pixel count and compression work in tandem to determine file size and image quality. Tons of pixels and minimum compression mean big files and maximum quality. Fewer pixels and maximum compression mean smaller files and lesser quality.

Selecting a file format

Some cameras enable you to select from a few different file formats — JPEG, TIFF, and so on. (Chapter 6 explains these and other file formats in detail.) Some cameras also provide a proprietary format — that is, a format unique to the camera — along with the more standard formats.

When deciding on a file format, consider these factoids:

✔ Some file formats result in larger image files than others because of the structure of the data in the file or the amount of compression that's applied.

If that sounds sort of vague, well, it is. I suggest that you shoot the same image using the different file formats available on your camera. Then transfer the pictures to your computer and compare the file size of each image. Now you know what format to use when you want to stuff the maximum number of images in your camera's available memory.

✔ The format you select may affect image quality. So give each of your test images a close-up inspection. Does one picture look sharper than the other? Is one a little jaggedy in areas where the other looks fine? When picture quality is a priority, choose the file format that gives you the best-looking images.

Keep in mind, though, that you pay for better picture quality with larger file sizes. For example, some cameras enable you to store images as TIFF files with no compression or as JPEG files with some compression. Although you undoubtedly get better image quality from the TIFF option, the number of pictures you can take before you fill up your available camera memory will be much lower than if you select JPEG.

✔ All other things being equal, choose a standard file format, such as JPEG or TIFF, over a camera's proprietary image format. Why? Because most proprietary formats aren't supported by image-editing and image-cataloguing programs. So before you can edit or catalogue your pictures, you have to take the extra step of converting them to a standard file format using the software that came with your camera.

If you're transferring your images to your computer using a cable connection, you can often perform the format conversion at the same time you download (check your camera's software manual for format information and see Chapter 6 for more information on this process). But if you're transferring pictures via a floppy disk, floppy-disk adapter, or memory-card reader, storing your images in a standard format rather than the proprietary format means that you can open the files on your disk or memory card immediately, without doing any conversion.

✔ A few cameras provide you with the option of storing images in the FlashPix file format. Developed a few years ago, FlashPix was once touted as the ideal solution for digital images. Although the concept behind FlashPix was intriguing, the format never took hold and appears now to be dead in its tracks. As a result, few cataloguing and image-editing programs can work with FlashPix files. So stay away from this format unless your software welcomes FlashPix files with open arms.

Balancing Your Whites and Colours

Different light sources have varying *colour temperatures,* which is a fancy way of saying that they contain different amounts of red, green, and blue light.

Colour temperature is measured in Kelvin degrees, a fact that you don't really need to remember unless you want to dish with experienced film or video photographers, who sometimes toss the term into their conversations. The midday sun has a colour temperature of about 5500 degrees Kelvin, which is often abbreviated as 5500°K — not to be confused with 5500 kilobytes, abbreviated as 5500K. When two worlds as full of technical lingo as photography and computers collide, havoc ensues. If you're ever unsure as to which *K* is being discussed, just nod your head thoughtfully and say, "Yes, I see your point."

Anyway, the colour temperature of the light source affects how a camera — video, digital, or film — perceives the colours of the objects being photographed. If you've taken pictures in fluorescent lighting, you may have noticed a slight green tint to your photographs. The tint comes from the colour of fluorescent light.

Film photographers use special films or lens filters designed to compensate for different light sources. But digital cameras, like video cameras, get around the colour-temperature problem using a process known as *white balancing.* White balancing simply tells the camera what combination of red, green, and blue light it should perceive as pure white, given the current lighting conditions. With that information as a baseline, the camera can then accurately reproduce all the other colours in the scene.

On most digital cameras, white balancing is handled automatically. But many higher-end models provide manual white-balance controls as well. Why would you want to make manual white-balance adjustments? Because sometimes, automatic white balancing doesn't go quite far enough in removing unwanted colour casts. If you notice that your whites aren't really white or that the image has an unnatural tint, you can sometimes correct the problem by choosing a different white-balance setting.

Typically, you can choose from the following manual settings:

- ✔ Daylight or Sunny, for shooting outdoors in bright light

- ✔ Cloudy, for shooting outdoors in overcast skies

- ✔ Fluorescent, for taking pictures in fluorescent lights, such as those found in office buildings

- ✔ Tungsten, for shooting under incandescent lights (standard household lights)

- ✔ Flash, for shooting with the camera's on-board flash

Although white-balance controls are designed to improve colour accuracy, some digital photographers use them to mimic the effects produced by traditional colour filters, such as a warming filter. You can get a variety of takes on the same scene simply by varying the white-balance setting. How each setting affects your image colours depends on the lighting conditions in your scene.

If your camera doesn't offer white-balance adjustment or you just forget to think about this issue when you're shooting, you can remove unwanted colour casts or give your picture a warmer or cooler tone in the photo-editing stage.

Composing for Compositing

For the most part, the rules of digital image composition are the same rules that film photographers have followed for years. But when you're creating digital images, you need to consider an additional factor: how the image will be used. If you want to be able to lift part of your picture out of its background — for example, in order to paste the subject into another image — pay special attention to the background and framing of the image.

Digital-imaging gurus refer to the process of combining two images as *compositing,* by the way.

Suppose that you're creating a product brochure and you want to create a photo montage that combines images of four products. To make life easier in the photo-editing stage, shoot each product against a plain background. That way, you can easily separate the product from the background when you're ready to cut and paste the product image into your montage.

You must *select* an element before you can lift it out of its background and paste it into another picture. Selecting simply draws an outline around the element so that the computer knows which pixels to cut and paste. So why does shooting your subject against a plain background make the job easier? Because most photo editors offer a tool that enables you to click a colour in your image to automatically select surrounding areas that are similarly coloured. If you shoot your subject against a red backdrop, for example, you can select the background by clicking on a red background pixel. You then can invert (reverse) the selection to easily select the subject.

If you shoot the object against a complex background, like the one in Figure 5-1, you lose this option. You have to draw your selection outline manually by tracing around it with your mouse. Selecting an image "by hand" is a fairly difficult proposition for most folks, especially when working with a mouse.

Figure 5-1: Avoid busy backgrounds such as this one when shooting objects that you plan to use in a photo collage.

Remember that if you want to separate an object from its background in the editing stage, shoot the object against a plain background, as in Figure 5-2. Make sure that the background colour is distinct from the colours around the *perimeter* of the subject, not the interior, if you have a multicolour subject such as the camera in Figure 5-2. I shot the camera against a dark background to provide the greatest contrast to the silver edges of the camera.

Figure 5-2: Shoot collage elements against a plain, contrasting background and fill as much of the frame as possible with the object.

Another important rule of shooting images for compositing is to fill as much of the frame as possible with your subject, as I did in Figure 5-2. That way, you devote the maximum number of pixels to your subject, rather than wasting them on a background that you're going to trim away. The more pixels you have, the better the print quality you can achieve. (See Chapter 2 for more information on this law of digital imaging.)

While we're on the subject of creating photographic collages, make it a point on your next photographic expedition to look for surfaces that you can use as backgrounds in your composite images. For example, a close-up of a nicely coloured marble tile or a section of weathered barn siding can serve as an interesting background in a montage.

Zooming In without Losing Out

Many digital cameras offer zoom lenses that enable you to get a close-up perspective on your subject without going to the bother of actually moving toward the subject.

Some cameras provide an *optical zoom,* which is a true zoom lens, just like the one you may have on your film camera. Other cameras offer a *digital zoom,* which isn't a zoom lens at all but a bit of pixel sleight of hand. The next two sections offer some guidelines for working with both types of zooms.

Shooting with an optical (real) zoom

If your camera has an optical zoom, keep these tips in mind before you trigger that zoom button or switch:

- ✔ The closer you get to your subject, the greater the chance of a parallax error. Chapter 4 explains this phenomenon fully, but in a nutshell, parallax errors cause the image you see in your viewfinder to be different from what your camera's lens sees and records. To make sure that you wind up with the picture you have in mind, frame your picture using the LCD monitor instead of the viewfinder. You can alternatively frame your subject using the framing marks in your viewfinder; check your camera's manual to find out which marks apply for zoom shooting.

- ✔ When you zoom in on a subject, you can fit less of the background into the frame than if you zoom out and get your close-up shot by moving nearer to the subject.

- ✔ Zooming to a telephoto setting also tends to make the background blurrier than if you shoot close to the subject. This happens because the *depth of field* changes when you zoom. Depth of field simply refers to the zone of sharp focus in your photo. With a short depth of field — which is what you get when you're zoomed in — elements that are close to the camera are sharply focused, but distant background elements are not. When you zoom to a wide-angle lens setting, you have a greater depth of field, so faraway objects may be as sharply focused as your main subject.

Keep in mind that varying the camera's aperture setting also affects depth of field.

Using a digital zoom

Some cameras put a new twist on zooming, providing a *digital zoom* rather than an optical zoom. With digital zoom, the camera enlarges the elements at the centre of the frame to create the *appearance* that you've zoomed in.

Say that you want to take a picture of a boat that's bobbing in the middle of a lake. You decide to zoom in on the boat and lose the watery surroundings. The camera crops out the lake pixels and magnifies the boat pixels to fill the frame. The end result is no different than if you had captured both boat and lake, cropped the lake away in your photo software, and then enlarged the remaining boat image. In addition, a digital zoom doesn't produce the same change in depth of field as an optical zoom. (See the preceding section for details on this issue.)

Given that a digital zoom doesn't provide anything you couldn't achieve in your photo software, why would you want to use it? To wind up with smaller image files, which means that you can fit more images in your camera's memory before you have to download. Because the camera is cropping away the pixels around the edge of the frame, you don't have to store those pixels in memory — just the ones devoted to your main subject. If you know that you don't want those extra pixels, go ahead and use the digital zoom. Otherwise, ignore the feature and do your cropping in your photo software.

Catching a Moving Target

Capturing action with most digital cameras isn't an easy proposition. As you may recall if you read Chapter 2, digital cameras need plenty of light to produce good images. Unless you're shooting in a very brightly lit setting, the shutter speed required to properly expose the image may be too slow to "stop" action — that is, to record a non-blurry image of a moving target.

Compounding the problem, the camera needs a few seconds to establish the autofocus and autoexposure settings before you shoot, plus a few seconds after you shoot to process and store the image in memory. If you're shooting with a flash, you also must give the flash a few seconds to recycle between pictures.

Some cameras offer a rapid-fire option, usually known as *burst mode* or *continuous capture mode,* that enables you to shoot a series of images with one press of the shutter button. The camera takes pictures at timed intervals as long as you keep the shutter button pressed. This feature eliminates some of the lag time that occurs from the moment you press the shutter button until the time you can take another picture. I used the burst mode on a Kodak digital camera to record the series of images in Figure 5-3.

If your camera offers burst-mode shooting, check to find out whether you can adjust the settings to capture more or fewer images within a set period of time. To capture the images in Figure 5-3, for example, I set the camera to its fastest burst mode, three frames per second.

Keep in mind that most cameras can shoot only low- or medium-resolution pictures in burst mode (high-resolution pictures would require a longer storage time). And the flash is typically disabled for this capture mode. More importantly, though, timing the shots so that you catch the height of the action is difficult. Notice that in Figure 5-3, I didn't capture the most important moment in the swing — the point at which the club makes contact with the ball! If you're interested in recording just one particular moment, you may be better off using a regular shooting mode so that you have better control over when each picture is taken.

When you're shooting action shots "the normal way" — that is, without the help of burst mode — use these tricks to do a better job of stopping a moving subject in its tracks:

✔ **Lock in focus and exposure in advance.** Press the shutter button halfway down to initiate the autofocus and auto-exposure process (if your camera offers these features) well ahead of the time when you want to capture the image. That way, when the action happens, you don't have to wait for the focus and exposure to be set. When locking in the focus and exposure, aim the camera at an

Figure 5-3: Burst mode enables you to shoot a moving target. Here, a
   capture setting of three frames per second broke a golfer's
   swing into six stages.

object or person approximately the same distance away and in the same lighting conditions as your final subject will be. See Chapter 4 for more information about locking in focus and exposure.

✔ Anticipate the shot. With just about any camera, there's a slight delay between the time you press the shutter button and the time the camera actually records the image. So the trick to catching action is to press the shutter button just a split second *before* the action occurs. Practise shooting with your camera until you have a feel for how far in advance you need to press that shutter button.

✔ Turn on the flash. Even if it's daylight, turning on the flash sometimes causes the camera to select a higher shutter speed, thereby freezing action better. To make sure that the flash is activated, use the fill-flash mode, discussed in Chapter 4, rather than auto-flash mode. Remember, though, that the flash may need time to recycle between shots. So for taking a series of action shots, you may want to turn the flash off.

✔ Switch to shutter-priority autoexposure mode (if available). Then select the highest shutter speed the camera provides and take a test shot. If the picture is too dark, lower the shutter speed a notch and retest. Remember, in shutter-priority mode, the camera reads the light in the scene and then sets the aperture as needed to properly expose the image at the shutter speed you select. So if the lighting isn't great, you may not be able to set the shutter speed high enough to stop action. For more about this issue, see Chapter 4.

✔ Use a lower capture resolution. The lower the capture resolution, the smaller the image file, and the less time the camera needs to record the image to memory. That means that you can take a second shot sooner than if you captured a high-resolution image.

✔ If your camera offers an "instant review" feature that automatically displays a picture on the LCD monitor for a few seconds after you shoot the image, turn off the feature. When it's on, the camera likely won't let you take another picture during the review period.

✔ Make sure that your camera batteries are fresh. Weak batteries can sometimes make your camera behave sluggishly.

✔ Keep the camera turned on. Because digital cameras suck up battery juice like nobody's business, the natural tendency is to turn off your camera between shots. But digital cameras take a few seconds to warm up after you turn them on — during which time, whatever it was that you were trying to record may have come and gone. Do turn the LCD monitor off, though, to conserve battery power.

Shooting Pieces of a Panoramic Quilt

You're standing at the edge of the Grand Canyon, awestruck by the colours, light, and majestic rock formations. "If only I could capture all this in a photograph!" you think. But when you view the scene through your camera's viewfinder, you quickly realize that you can't possibly do justice to such a magnificent landscape with one ordinary picture.

Wait — don't put down that camera and head for the souvenir shack just yet. When you're shooting digitally, you don't have to try to squeeze the entire canyon — or whatever other subject inspires you — into one frame. You can shoot several frames, each featuring a different part of the scene, and then stitch them together just as you would sew together pieces of a patchwork quilt. Figure 5-4 shows two images of a historic farmhouse that I stitched together into the panorama shown in Figure 5-5.

Figure 5-4: I stitched together these two images to create the panorama in Figure 5-5.

Figure 5-5: The resulting panorama provides a larger perspective on the farmhouse scene.

Although you could conceivably combine photos into a panorama using your image-editor's regular cut-and-paste editing tools, a dedicated stitching tool makes the job easier. You simply pull up the images you want to join, and the program assists you in stitching the digital "seam."

Some camera manufacturers provide proprietary stitching tools as part of the camera's software bundle. In addition, many photo-editing programs offer a stitching tool. You also can buy stand-alone stitching programs such as ArcSoft Panorama Maker (www.arcsoft.com) and Photovista Panorama, from iSeeMedia (www.iseemedia.com).

The stitching process is easy if you shoot the original images correctly. If you don't, you wind up with something that looks more like a crazy quilt than a seamless photographic panorama. Here's what you need to know:

✔ You must capture each picture using the same camera-to-subject distance and camera height. If you're shooting a wide building, don't get closer to the building at one end than you do at another, for example, or raise the camera for one shot in the series.

✔ Each shot should overlap the previous shot by at least 30 percent. Say that you're shooting a line of ten cars. If image one includes the first three cars in the line, image two should include the third car as well as cars four and five. Some cameras provide a panorama mode that displays a portion of the previous shot in the monitor so that you can see where to align the next shot in the series.

If your camera doesn't offer this feature, you need to make a mental note of where each picture ends so that you know where the next picture should begin.

✔ As you pan the camera to capture the different shots in the panorama, imagine that the camera is perched atop a short flagpole, with the camera's lens aligned with the pole. Be sure to use that same alignment as you take each shot. If you don't keep the same axis of rotation throughout your shots, you can't successfully join the images later. For best results, use a tripod.

✔ Keeping the camera level is equally important. Some tripods include little bubble levels that help you keep the camera on an even keel. If you don't have this kind of tripod, you may want to buy a little stick-on level at the hardware store and put it on top of your camera.

✔ Use a consistent focusing approach. If you lock the focus on the foreground in one shot, don't focus on the background in the next shot.

✔ Check your camera manual to find out whether your camera offers an exposure lock function. This feature retains a consistent exposure throughout the series of panorama shots, which is important for seamless image stitching.

If your camera doesn't provide a way to override auto-exposure, you may need to fool the camera into using a consistent exposure. Say that one half of a scene is in the shadows and the other is in the sunlight. With autoexposure enabled, the camera increases the exposure for the shadowed area and decreases the exposure for the sunny area. That sounds like a good thing, but what it really does is create a noticeable colour shift between the two halves of the picture. To prevent this problem, lock in the focus and exposure on the same point for each shot. Choose a point of medium brightness for best results.

✔ Be aware of people, cars, and other objects that may be moving in the background, and try to avoid including them in your shots. If a person is walking across the landscape you're trying to shoot, you wind up with the same strolling figure in each frame of the panorama!

If you really enjoy creating panorama images or need to do so regularly for business purposes, you can make your life a little easier by investing in a product such as the Kaidan KiWi+ Panoramic Tripod Head, showing in Figure 5-6. This tripod attachment helps you make sure that each shot is perfectly set up to create a seamless panorama. The KiWi+ sells for about $300 (www.kaidan.com).

Figure 5-6: Specialized tripod attachments such as the Kaidan KiWi+ make shooting seamless panoramic images easier.

Photographers with even bigger budgets may want to consider so-called *one-shot panorama tools,* which capture all the pictures needed to create a 360-degree panoramic image with one press of the shutter button. Expect to pay over $1,000 for such tools, offered by Kaidan and a few other manufacturers.

Avoiding the Digital Measles

Are your images coming out of your camera looking a little blotchy or dotted with coloured speckles? Do some parts of the image have a jagged appearance? If so, the following remedies can cure your pictures:

✔ Use a lower compression setting. Jaggedy or blotchy images are often the result of too much compression. Check your camera manual to find out how to choose a lower compression setting.

✔ Raise the resolution. Too few pixels can mean blocky-looking — or pixelated — images. The larger you print the photo, the worse the problem becomes. (See Chapter 2 for information on why low resolution translates to poor print quality.)

✔ Increase the lighting. Photos shot in very low light often take on a grainy appearance, like the one in Figure 5-7.

✔ Lower the camera's ISO setting (if possible). Typically, the higher the ISO, the grainier the image. For more on this issue, check out Chapter 4.

Figure 5-7: Low lighting can result in grainy images.

Part III
From Camera to Computer and Beyond

The 5th Wave   By Rich Tennant

"Ooo-wait! That's perfect for the clinic's home page. Just stretch it out a little further... little more... "

In this part...

One major advantage of digital photography is how quickly you can go from camera to final output. In minutes, you can print or electronically distribute your images, while your film-based friends are cooling their heels, waiting for their pictures to be developed at the one-hour photo lab.

The chapters in this part of the book contain everything you need to know to get your pictures out of your camera and into the hands of friends, relatives, clients, or anyone else. Chapter 6 explains the process of transferring images to your computer and also discusses various ways to store image files. And Chapter 7 explores electronic distribution of images — placing them on the World Wide Web, sharing them via e-mail, and the like — and offers ideas for additional on-screen uses for your images.

In other words, you find out how to coax all the pretty pixels inside your camera to come out of hiding and reveal your photographic genius to the world.

Chapter 6

Building Your Image Warehouse

- -

In This Chapter

▶ Downloading photos from the camera to your computer

▶ Importing pictures directly into a photo-editing or catalogue program

▶ Viewing photos on a TV and recording pictures on videotape

▶ Choosing an image file format to use

▶ Organizing your picture files

- -

Maybe you're a highly organized photographer. As soon as you bring home prints from the photofinisher, you sort them according to date or subject matter, slip them into a photo album, and neatly record the date the picture was shot, the negative number, and the place where the negative is stored.

Then again, maybe you're like the rest of us — full of good intentions about organizing your life, but never quite finding the time to do it. I, for one, currently have no fewer than ten packets of pictures strewn about my house, all waiting patiently for their turn to make it into an album. Were you to ask me for a reprint of one of those pictures, you'd no doubt go to your grave waiting for me to deliver, because the odds that I'd be able to find the matching negative are absolutely zilch.

If you and I are soul mates on this issue, I have unfortunate news for you: Digital photography demands that you devote some time to organizing and cataloguing images after you download them to your computer. If you don't, you'll have a tough time finding specific photos when you need them. With digital photos, you can't flip through a stack of prints to find a particular shot — you have to use a photo editor or viewer to look at each picture. Unless you set up some sort of orderly cataloguing system, you waste a *lot* of time opening and closing image files before you find the picture you want.

Before you can catalogue your photos, of course, you have to move them from the camera to the computer. This chapter gives you a look at the picture-downloading process, explains the file formats you can use when saving your images, and introduces you to image-cataloguing software. By the end of this chapter, you'll be so organized that you may even be motivated to tackle that closet in your bedroom.

Downloading Your Images

You've got a camera full of pictures. Now what? You transfer them to your computer, that's what. The following sections introduce you to several methods of doing so.

Some digital photography aficionados refer to the process of moving photos from the camera to the computer as *downloading,* by the way.

A trio of downloading options

Digital camera manufacturers have developed several ways for users to transfer pictures from camera to computer. You may or may not be able to use all these options, depending on your camera. The following list outlines the various transfer methods, beginning with the fastest and easiest choice:

✔ **Memory card transfer:** If your camera stores images on a floppy disk, just pop the disk out of your camera and insert it into the floppy drive on your computer. Then copy the images to your hard drive as you do regular data files on a floppy disk.

If your camera uses CompactFlash, SmartMedia, Memory Stick, or some other type of removable storage media, you can also enjoy the convenience of transferring images directly from that media, provided you have a matching card reader or adapter. See Chapter 3 for more information on these gadgets.

✔ **Cable transfer:** If you don't have the luxury of using the preceding transfer option, you're stuck with the "old-fashioned" method, which is to connect your computer and camera using the cable that came in your camera box.

In some cases, the connection is via a serial cable, which transfers data at a speed roughly equivalent to a turtle pulling a 2-ton pickup. Okay, so maybe the speed isn't quite that slow — it just seems that way. Fortunately, most newer cameras connect to the computer via a USB port, which makes the transfer process faster.

The steps in the next section explain the transfer process, whether you use serial or USB cabling.

✔ **Infrared transfer:** A few cameras have an IrDA port that enables you to transfer files via infrared light beams, similar to the way your TV remote control transfers your channel-surfing commands to your TV set. In order to use this feature, your computer must have an IrDA port.

In case you're curious, IrDA stands for Infrared Data Association, an organization of electronics manufacturers that sets technical standards for devices that use infrared transfer. These standards ensure that the IrDA port on one vendor's equipment can talk to the IrDA port on another vendor's equipment.

Having tried IrDA transfer, I can tell you that getting the communication settings just right can be a challenge. I had the help of two tech support people (one for my laptop and one for the camera I was using), and between the three of us, getting the system working took well over an hour — basically, we just kept playing with different options until we stumbled across the right combinations. Maybe you'll have better luck.

If you do manage to get your camera and computer to communicate via IrDA, you simply place your camera close to your computer and start the camera's transfer program. Your image-transfer speed depends on the capabilities of your computer's IrDA port. With my laptop, the transfer rate was no faster than using a serial-cable connection (see the preceding bullet point).

Different IrDA devices work differently, so consult your camera and computer manuals to find out how to take advantage of this option.

Regardless of which transfer method you use, don't forget to install the image-transfer software that came with your camera. If you're using direct memory card-to-computer transfer and your camera saves images in a standard file format (such as TIFF or JPEG), you may not need the software; you can open your images directly from the card (or other removable media) in your photo-editing program. But some cameras store images in a proprietary format that can be read only by the camera's transfer software. Before you can open the pictures in a photo-editing program, you have to convert them to a standard format using the camera transfer software. (See "File Format Free-for-All," later in this chapter, for an explanation of file formats.)

Cable transfer how-tos

Transferring photos via a camera-to-computer connection works pretty much the same way from model to model. Because transfer software differs substantially from camera to camera, I can't give you specific commands for accessing your photos; check your camera's manual for that information. But in general, the process works as outlined in the following steps. (I'm assuming that you're not working with one of the new camera docks that stays connected to your computer while you're off shooting pictures. For more on these devices, see Chapter 3.)

Note that the first time you connect your camera and computer, you may need to do so in a special way and install some software that came with the camera. Again, dig out that camera manual for specifics.

With the proper software installed, the transfer process works like so:

1. If you're connecting via serial cable, turn off your computer and camera.

This step is *essential;* most cameras don't support *hot swapping* — connecting via serial cable while the devices are turned on. If you connect the camera to the computer while either machine is powered up, you risk damaging the camera.

2. **If you're connecting via USB, check your camera manual.**

You probably do not have to shut down your computer before hooking up the camera. But please, check your camera and computer manuals to be certain. You may or may not need to turn the camera off.

3. **Connect the camera to your computer.**

Plug one end of the connection cable into your camera and the other into your computer. If you're going the serial-cable route and you use a Macintosh computer, you typically plug the camera cable into the printer or modem port, as shown in the top half of Figure 6-1. On a PC, the serial cable usually connects to a COM port (often used for connecting external modems to the computer), as shown in the bottom half of Figure 6-1.

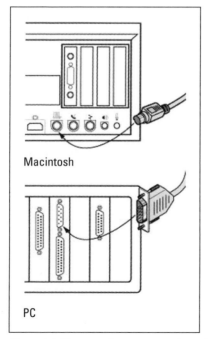

Macintosh

PC

Figure 6-1: If connecting a camera via serial cable, you usually plug the cable into the printer or modem port on a Mac and into a COM port on a PC.

Mac or Windows — does it matter?

Here's a relatively easy one. Most — not all, but most — digital cameras work on both Macintosh and Windows-based computers. The only differences lie in the cabling that hooks the camera to your computer and the software that you use to download and edit your pictures. Most cameras come with the appropriate cabling and software for both platforms, although you should verify this before making your final selection. Of course, if the camera stores pictures on removable memory cards, you can always buy a memory card reader and eliminate the need to connect camera and computer altogether. (See Chapter 3 for more about this option.)

Nor do you need to worry that your Mac friends won't be able to open and view your digital photos if you work on a PC, or vice versa. Several image file formats work on both platforms, and you can buy good image-editing programs for both, too, although the choices for Macintosh software are more limited than on the Windows side. Check out the "File Format Free-for-All" section later in this chapter if you want more details about file formats, and spend a minute or two with Chapter 3 for tips on choosing software.

A few cameras that operate on the Windows platform require computers with a Pentium II or MMX processor or better. And Windows 95 usually doesn't cooperate with cameras that connect to the computer via a USB cable, even if you use the version of Windows 95 that's supposed to enable USB. So before buying a camera, check to see whether your computer matches the camera's system requirements.

The step is the same for cameras that come with a USB cable. Plug one end of the cable into the camera and the other into your computer's USB port.

Note that if you use Windows 95, your computer may refuse to recognize the presence of the camera, even if you install the Windows 95 update that is supposed to enable USB. So if you want to avoid hassles, either upgrade to a later version of Windows or use some method of image transfer other than USB.

4. **Turn the computer and camera back on, if you turned them off before connecting.**

5. **Set the camera to the appropriate mode for image transfer.**

On some cameras, you put the camera in playback mode; other cameras have a PC setting. Check your manual to find out the right setting for your model.

6. **Start the image-transfer software.**

7. **Download away.**

From here on out, the commands and steps needed to get those pictures from your camera onto your computer vary, depending on the camera and transfer software.

Take the bullet TWAIN

Chances are good that your camera comes with a CD that enables you to install something called a *TWAIN driver* on your computer. TWAIN is a special *protocol* (language) that enables your photo-editing or catalogue program to communicate directly with a digital camera or scanner. Rumour has it that TWAIN stands for Technology Without An Interesting Name. Those wacky computer people!

After you install the TWAIN driver, you can access picture files that are still on the camera through your photo-editing or cataloguing program. Of course, your camera still needs to be cabled to the computer. And your photo-editing or cataloguing program must be *TWAIN-compliant,* meaning that it understands the TWAIN language.

The command you use to open camera images varies from program to program. Typically, the command is found in the File menu and is named something like Acquire or Import. (In some programs, you first have to select the *TWAIN source* — that is, specify which piece of hardware you want to access. This command is also usually found in the File menu.)

Camera as hard drive

With some digital cameras, the manufacturer provides special software that, when installed on your computer, makes your computer think that the camera is just another hard drive. When you connect the camera to a Windows-based PC, for example, the camera gets its own little drive icon in Windows Explorer. On a Macintosh, the Finder displays the camera icon.

Whatever the operating system, you can double-click the camera icon to display a list of files in the camera, just as you would to review files on your other drives. Then you can drag and drop files from the camera to a location on your hard drive, an option that's typically quicker than downloading the individual images via the camera's transfer software.

How this feature works — if at all — depends on the version of Windows or Macintosh operating system you use, as well as on your camera. Check your camera's manual for details.

Tips for trouble-free downloads

For whatever reason, the download process is one of the more complicated aspects of digital photography. The introduction of direct memory-card-to-computer transfer has made things much easier, but not all users have access to this method. If you're transferring images via a serial cable, USB, or IrDA, don't feel badly if you run into problems — I do this stuff on a daily basis, and I still sometimes have trouble getting the download process to run smoothly when I work with a new camera. The problem isn't helped by camera manuals that provide little, if any, assistance on how to get your camera to talk to your computer.

Here are some troubleshooting tips I've picked up during my struggles with image transfer:

- ✔ If you get a message saying that the software can't communicate with the camera, check to make sure that the camera is turned on and set to the right mode (playback, PC mode, and so on).

- ✔ On a Macintosh, you may need to turn off AppleTalk, Express Modem, and/or GlobalFax, which can conflict with the transfer software. Check the camera manual for possible problem areas.

- ✔ On a PC, check the COM port setting in the transfer software if you have trouble getting the camera and computer to talk to each other via a serial cable connection. Make sure that the port selected in the download program is the one into which you plugged the camera.

✔ If you're connecting via a USB port, make sure that the USB port is enabled in your system. Some manufacturers ship their computers with the port disabled. To find out how to turn the thing on, check your computer manual. Also see my earlier comments about USB and Windows 95 in the section "Cable transfer how-tos."

✔ If your camera has an AC adapter, use it when downloading images via a serial cable. The process can take quite a while, and you need to conserve all the battery power you can for your photography outings.

✔ Check your camera manufacturer's Web site for trouble-shooting information. Manufacturers often post updated software drivers on their Web sites to address downloading problems. Log on to the Web sites for your brand of computer and image software, too, because problems may be related to that end of the download process rather than to your camera.

✔ Some transfer programs give you the option of choosing an image file format and compression setting for your transferred images. Unless you want to lose some image data — which results in lower image quality — choose the no-compression setting or use a lossless-compression scheme, such as LZW for TIFF images. (If that last sentence sounded like complete gibberish, you can find a translation in the section "File Format Free-for-All," later in this chapter. Also check out the section on compression settings in Chapter 5.)

✔ When you initiate the transfer process, you may be able to select an option that automatically deletes all images from the camera's memory after downloading. At the risk of sounding paranoid, I *never* select this option. After you transfer images, always review them on your computer monitor *before* you delete any images from your camera. Glitches can happen, so make sure that you really have that image on your computer before you wipe it off your camera. As an extra precaution, make a backup copy of the image on removable media (CD, Zip, or the like).

✔ Digital cameras typically assign your picture files meaningless names such as DCS008.jpg and DCS009.jpg (for PC files) or Image 1, Image 2, and the like (for Mac files). If you previously downloaded images and haven't renamed them, files by the same names as the ones you're downloading may already exist on your hard drive. When you attempt to transfer files, the computer should alert you to this fact and ask whether you want to replace the existing images with the new images. But just in case, you may want to create a new folder to hold the new batch of images before you download. That way, there's no chance that any existing images will be overwritten.

Now Playing on Channel 3

If you've shopped for a DVD player recently, you may have spotted an interesting new feature on a few models: A slot that accepts some types of digital camera media. You can pop a memory card out of your camera, insert the card into the DVD player, and view all the pictures on the card on your television set.

For those without the latest in home electronics technology, many cameras come with a *video-out* port and video connection cable. Translated into English, you can connect the camera itself to a DVD player or regular old TV to display your digital photos. You can even connect the camera to a VCR and record your images on videotape.

Why would you want to display your images on a TV? You can show your pictures to a group of people in your living room or office conference room instead of having them huddle around your computer monitor. Viewing your images on TV also enables you to review your images more closely than you can on your camera's LCD monitor. Small defects that may not be noticeable on the camera monitor become readily apparent when viewed on a 27-inch television screen.

As with connecting the camera to a computer, consult your camera's manual for specific instructions on how to hook your camera to the DVD player, TV, or VCR. Typically, you plug one end of an AV cable (supplied with the camera) into the camera's video- or AV-out port and then plug the other end into the video-in port on your TV, DVD player, or VCR. If your camera has audio-recording capabilities, the cable has a separate AV plug for the audio signal. That plug goes into the audio-in port. If your playback device supports stereo sound, you typically plug the camera's audio plug into the mono-input port.

To display your pictures on the TV, you generally use the same procedure as when reviewing your pictures on the camera's LCD monitor, but again, check your manual. To record the images on videotape, just put the VCR in record mode, turn on the camera, and display each image for the length of time you want to record it. You may need to select a different input source for the VCR or TV — for example, to switch the VCR from its standard antenna or cable input setting to its auxiliary input setting.

Most digital cameras sold in North America output video in NTSC format, which is the format used by televisions in North America. You can't display NTSC images on televisions in Europe and other countries that use the PAL format instead of NTSC. So if you're an international business mogul needing to display your images abroad, you may not be able to do it using your camera's video-out feature. Some newer cameras do provide you with the choice of NTSC or PAL formats.

File Format Free-for-All

You may be asked to choose a file format when you transfer images from your camera to your computer or when you set up the camera itself — many new cameras can store images in two or more different file formats. You also need to specify a file format in order to save your image after editing it in your image-editing software. (See Chapter 8 for more information on editing and saving files.)

The term _file format_ simply refers to a way of storing computer data. Many different image formats exist, and each one takes a unique approach to data storage. Some formats are _proprietary,_ which means that they're used only by the camera you're using. (Proprietary formats are sometimes also referred to as _native_ formats.)

If you want to edit photos stored in a proprietary format, you must use the software provided with the camera. Typically, you can use that software to convert the photo files to a format that can be opened by other programs.

Many photo-editing programs also have a proprietary format. Adobe Photoshop and Photoshop Elements, for example, use the PSD format, which supports all the editing features available in those programs and speeds editing inside each program. If you want to open the file in another program that doesn't support the PSD format, you can *export* the file to another format — that is, save a copy in that other format.

Some formats are used only on the Mac, and some formats are for PCs only. A few formats are so obscure that almost no one uses them anymore, while others have become so popular that almost every program on both platforms supports them. The following sections detail the most common file formats for storing images, along with the pros and cons of each format.

JPEG

Say it *jay-peg.* The acronym stands for Joint Photographic Experts Group, which was the organization that developed this format.

JPEG is one of the most widely used formats today, and almost every program, on both Macintosh and Windows systems, can save and open JPEG images. JPEG is also one of the two main file formats used for photos on the World Wide Web. Most digital cameras also store photos in this format.

One of the biggest advantages of JPEG is that it can compress image data, which results in smaller picture files. Smaller files consume less space on disk and take less time to download on the Web.

The catch is that JPEG uses a *lossy compression scheme,* which means that some image data is sacrificed during the compression process. For initial storage of pictures in camera memory, you don't lose too much data if you select a capture option that applies a minimal or medium amount of compression. But each time you open, edit, and resave your photo in your photo editor, the image is recompressed, and more damage is done.

When you save a file in the JPEG format, you can specify how much compression you want to apply, which makes sense because compression directly affects photo quality. To keep data loss to a minimum and ensure the best images, choose the highest-quality setting (which results in the least amount of compression). For Web images, you can get away with a medium-quality, medium-compression setting. For details on saving photos for use on the Web, see Chapter 7.

While you're working on a picture, save it in your photo-editing program's native format or the TIFF format (explained shortly), which retains all critical image data. Save to JPEG only when you've finished editing the image. That way, you keep data loss to a minimum.

EXIF

EXIF, which stands for *Exchangeable Image Format,* is one of many variants of the JPEG format. Many digital cameras store images using EXIF, sometimes referred to as JPEG (EXIF), to take advantage of the opportunity to store *metadata* — extra data — with the image file. In the case of digital cameras, information such as the shutter speed, aperture, and other capture settings gets recorded as metadata.

If your camera records metadata, you don't need to do anything different while capturing images, but you do need to use a special EXIF *extractor* program if you want to view the metadata after you download the pictures. Some cameras ship with proprietary software for viewing the metadata; you can also buy inexpensive programs to take a look. Two examples are Picture Information Extractor and ThumbsPlus, featured in the last section of this chapter.

One caveat regarding EXIF data: If you open your original picture file and resave it inside a photo-editing program, the metadata may be stripped from the file. If you're concerned with retaining metadata, always work on a copy of the original picture file.

TIFF

TIFF stands for *Tagged Image File Format,* in case you care, which you really shouldn't. TIFF — say it *tiff,* as in a little spat — ranks right up there with JPEG on the popularity scale except for use on the World Wide Web.

Like JPEG images, TIFF images can be opened by most Macintosh and Windows programs. If you need to bring a digital photo into a publishing program (such as Microsoft Publisher) or into a word processing program, TIFF is a good choice.

When you save an image to the TIFF format inside a photo editor, you're usually presented with a dialogue box containing a few options.

The most common TIFF option is *byte order.* If you want to use the image on a Mac, choose Macintosh; otherwise, select IBM PC. You also usually get the choice of applying LZW compression. LZW is a *lossless compression scheme,* which means that only redundant image data is abandoned when the image is compressed so that there is no loss in image quality.

Unfortunately, compressing an image in this way doesn't reduce the image file size as much as using JPEG compression, which is why TIFF isn't used on the Web and isn't supported by most Web browsers. (Most e-mail programs can't display TIFF images, either.)

 Most, but not all, photo-editing and publishing programs support LZW-compressed TIFF images. If you have trouble opening a TIFF image, compression may be the problem. Try opening and resaving the image in another program, this time turning compression off.

Some programs offer a few additional TIFF options, including the ability to apply JPEG compression. Unless you know what you're doing, leave these options at their default settings because they can cause the same file-opening problems as LZW compression. (And after all, if you're going to apply JPEG compression, what's the point of saving in the TIFF format in the first place?)

In addition to saving your picture as a TIFF file inside a photo editor, you may be able to set your camera to record TIFF images instead of JPEG files. Choose TIFF when picture quality is more important than file size — you can always make a copy of the picture in the JPEG format later if you want to use it on the Web.

RAW

High-resolution digital cameras aimed at serious photo enthusiasts often enable the user to capture pictures in the RAW file format as well as in JPEG and, sometimes, TIFF.

Unlike most computer terms, RAW isn't an acronym for anything — it simply means *raw,* as in *unprocessed* or *untouched.* Of course, when writing about the format, you have to capitalize it just for good technical measure.

When you capture a digital photo as a RAW file, any in-camera processing that's normally done to the picture files isn't applied. That includes sharpening, white balance, and other corrections that your camera may do automatically.

Some purists like RAW because it theoretically provides a truer version of the scene in front of the camera lens. However, RAW has some significant drawbacks. First, RAW files are substantially larger than JPEG files, although usually not as large as TIFF files. Second, many photo-editing and image-browsing programs can't open RAW files without a special plug-in (software add-on). Web browsers can't display RAW images, period, and you can't import RAW files into many other programs, including word processing programs, either.

If your digital camera offers the RAW format option, the manufacturer probably provides special software for viewing the picture files and converting them to a more common file format. Each manufacturer's version of RAW is slightly different, so you're likely locked into using your camera's software for these tasks.

Photo CD

Developed by Eastman Kodak, Photo CD is a format used expressly for transferring slides and film negatives onto a CD-ROM. Image-editing and cataloguing programs can open Photo CD images. But no consumer software enables you to save to this format; if you want to store pictures as Photo CD images, you must enlist the help of a commercial imaging lab.

The Photo CD format stores the same image at five different sizes, from 128 x 192 pixels all the way up to 2048 x 3072 pixels. The Pro Photo CD format, geared to those professionals who need ultra-high-resolution images, saves one additional size: 4096 x 6144 pixels.

When you open a Photo CD image, you can select which image size you want to use. Choose the size that corresponds to the number of pixels you need for your final output. For images that you plan to print, you generally want to select the largest size available. Remember that the more pixels in the image, the higher the image resolution and the better your printed output. If your computer complains that it doesn't have enough memory to open the image, try the next smaller size. For Web images, you can go with one of the smaller image sizes. (To read more about resolution, see Chapter 2.)

Many people confuse Photo CD with Picture CD, which isn't a file format at all, but a Kodak photofinishing offering. When you get your film developed at some photofinishers and request the Picture CD option, you receive regular prints plus a CD-ROM that contains scanned copies of your pictures. The pictures are stored on the CD in the JPEG format, and you open them as you do any JPEG image file.

GIF

Some people pronounce this format *gif,* with a hard *g,* while other folks say *jif,* like the peanut butter. I prefer the former, but you do what makes you happy. Either way, GIF was developed to facilitate transmission of images on CompuServe bulletin-board services.

Today, GIF *(Graphics Interchange Format)* and JPEG are the two most widely accepted formats for World Wide Web use. One variety of GIF, thoughtfully named GIF89a, enables you to make areas of your image transparent, so that your Web page background is visible through the image. You can also produce animated Web graphics using a series of GIF images.

GIF is similar to TIFF in that it uses LZW compression, which creates smaller file sizes without dumping any important image data. The drawback is that GIF is limited to saving 8-bit images (256 colours or less). What this limitation can mean is that your colour images have a rough, blotchy appearance because there aren't enough different colours available to express all the original shades in the image. For example, one shade of yellow must be used to represent several different yellow tones. For information on converting your image to 256 colours and creating a transparent GIF image, see Chapter 7.

PNG

PNG, which stands for *Portable Network Graphics* format and is pronounced *ping,* is a relatively new format designed for Web graphics. Unlike GIF, PNG isn't limited to 256 colours, and unlike JPEG, PNG doesn't use lossy compression. The upside is that you get better image quality; the downside is that your file sizes are larger, which means longer download times for Web surfers wanting to view your images. More problematic than that drawback, though, is the fact that people viewing your Web pages with older browsers may not be able to display PNG images. For now, GIF and JPEG are better options for Web use.

BMP

Some people pronounce this one by saying the letters (B-M-P), while other folks use *bimp* or *bump,* and still others avoid the whole issue by using the official name of the format, *Windows Bitmap.* A popular format in the past, BMP is used today primarily for images that will be used as wallpaper on PCs running Windows. Programmers sometimes also use BMP for images that will appear in Help systems.

BMP offers a lossless compression scheme known as RLE (Run-Length Encoding), which is a fine option except when you're creating a wallpaper image file. Windows sometimes has trouble recognizing files saved with RLE when searching for wallpaper images, so you may need to turn RLE off for this use.

PICT

When talking about this format, say *pict,* as in *Peter Piper PICT a peck of pixels.* PICT is based on the Apple QuickDraw screen language and is the native graphics format for Macintosh computers.

If QuickTime is installed on your Mac, you can apply JPEG compression to PICT images. But be aware that QuickTime's version of JPEG compression does slightly more damage to your image than what you get when you save it as a regular JPEG file. Because of this, saving your file to JPEG is a better option than PICT in most cases. About the only reason to use

PICT is to enable someone who doesn't have image-editing software to see your images. You can open PICT files inside SimpleText, Microsoft Word, and other word processors.

EPS

EPS (*Encapsulated PostScript,* pronounced *E-P-S*) is a format used mostly for high-end desktop publishing and graphics production work. If your desktop publishing program or commercial service bureau requires EPS, go ahead and use it. Otherwise, choose TIFF or JPEG. EPS files take up much more room on disk than TIFF and JPEG files.

Photo Organization Tools

After you move all those picture files from your camera to your hard drive, a CD, or other image warehouse, you need to organize them so that you can easily find a particular photo.

If you're a no-frills type of person, you can simply organize your picture files into folders, as you do your word-processing files, spreadsheets, and other documents. You may keep all pictures shot during a particular year or month in one folder, with images segregated into subfolders by subject. For example, your main folder may be named Photos, and your subfolders may be named Family, Sunsets, Holidays, Work, and so on.

Many photo-editing programs include a utility that enables you to browse through your image files and view thumbnails of each photo. Such file browser utilities make it easy to track down a particular image if you can't quite remember what you named the thing.

Depending on your computer's operating system, it also may offer tools for browsing through thumbnails of your digital photo files. Recent versions of Windows, for example, enable you to view thumbnails in Windows Explorer. If you work on a Macintosh computer running OS X 10.1.2 or later, you can download a free copy of a photo browser called iPhoto at the Apple Web site.

You may find that your operating system or photo editing program together offer all the image-file viewing and management tools that you need. But in many cases, these tools are very limited, slow, or both. If you have a large photo collection, the job of managing your picture files becomes much easier with stand-alone image-management programs such as ThumbsPlus (www.thumbsplus.com), shown in Figure 6-2.

You can browse and manage your images in several different layouts, including one that mimics the Windows Explorer format, as shown in Figure 6-2. In the latest version of this program, you also can inspect all the EXIF metadata that your camera may store in the image file.

But the real power of programs such as ThumbsPlus lies in their database features, which you can use to assign keywords to images and then search for files using those keywords. For example, if you have an image of a Labrador retriever, you might assign the keywords "dog" and "retriever" to the picture's catalogue information. When you run a search, entering any of those keywords as search criteria brings up the image. ThumbsPlus also enables you to perform some limited image editing and create a Web page that features your pictures.

Geared to more casual use, programs such as FlipAlbum Suite (www.flipalbum.com) feature a traditional photo-album motif. Figure 6-3 offers a look at this program. You drag images from a browser onto album pages, where you can then label the images and record information, such as the date and place the image was shot.

Photo-album programs are great for those times when you want to leisurely review your images or show them to others, much as you would enjoy a traditional photo album. And creating a digital photo album can be a fun project to enjoy with your kids — they'll love picking out frames for images and adding other special effects. In addition, some album programs, including FlipAlbum Suite, offer tools to help you create and share CDs containing your digital photo albums.

For simply tracking down a specific image or organizing images into folders, however, I prefer the folder-type approach like the one used by ThumbsPlus. I find that design quicker and easier to use than flipping through the pages of a digital photo album.

Figure 6-2: ThumbsPlus is a popular tool for viewing and organizing digital photo files.

Figure 6-3: You can use programs such as FlipAlbum Suite to create digital photo albums.

Chapter 7

On-Screen, Mr. Sulu!

*D*igital cameras are ideal for creating pictures for on-screen display. Even the most inexpensive, entry-level cameras can deliver enough pixels to create good images for Web pages, online photo albums, multimedia presentations, and other on-screen uses.

The process of preparing your pictures for the screen can be a little confusing, however, in part because so many people don't understand the correct approach and keep passing along bad advice to newcomers.

This chapter shows you how to do things the right way. You find out how to set the display size of on-screen photos, which file formats work best for different uses, how to send a picture along with an e-mail message, and more.

Step into the Screening Room

With a printed picture, your display options are fairly limited. You can pop the thing into a frame or photo album. You can stick it to a refrigerator with one of those annoyingly cute refrigerator magnets. Or you can slip it into your wallet so that you're prepared when an acquaintance inquires after you and yours.

In their digital state, however, photos can be displayed in all sorts of new and creative ways, including the following:

✔ **Add pictures to your company's site on the Web.** Many folks these days even have personal Web pages devoted not to selling products but to sharing information about themselves. See "Nothing but Net: Photos on the Web," later in this chapter, for details on preparing a digital photo for use on a Web page.

✔ **E-mail a picture** to friends, clients, or relatives, who then can view the image on their computer screens, save the image to disk, and even edit and print the photo. Check out "Drop Me a Picture Sometime, Won't You?" later in this chapter for information on how to attach a picture to your next e-mail missive.

✔ Alternatively, **create an online album** through a photo-sharing site such as the Black's Online PhotoCentre (www.blackphoto.com). After uploading pictures, you can invite people to view your album and to buy prints of their favourite photos.

Figure 7-1 offers a look at an online album that was created at the Black's Web site to share pictures of a recent golfing vacation.

✔ **Import the picture into a multimedia presentation program** such as Microsoft PowerPoint or Corel Presentations. The right images, displayed at the right time, can add excitement and emotional impact to your presentations and also clarify your ideas. Check your presentation program's manual for specifics on how to add a digital photo to your next show.

✔ **Create a personalized screen saver** featuring your favourite images. Most consumer photo-editing programs include a wizard or utility that makes creating such a screen saver easy.

✔ **With many digital cameras, you can download images to your TV, DVD player, or VCR.** You can then show your pictures to a living room full of captive guests and even record your images to videotape. Load up the camera with close-up pictures of your navel, cable the camera to your TV, and you've got an evening that's every bit as effective as an old-time slide show for convincing pesky neighbours that they should never set foot in your house again. For information on this intriguing possibility, see Chapter 6.

Figure 7-1: Online album sites such as the Black's Online PhotoCentre offer a convenient way to share photos with far-flung friends and relatives.

That's About the Size of It

Preparing pictures for on-screen display requires a different approach than you use to get them ready for the printer. The following sections tell all.

Understanding monitor resolution and picture size

As you prepare pictures for on-screen use, remember that monitors display images using one screen pixel for every image pixel. (If you need a primer on pixels, flip back to Chapter 2.) The exception is when you're working in a photo-editing program or other application that enables you to zoom in on a picture, thereby devoting several screen pixels to each image pixel.

Most monitors can be set to a choice of displays, each of which results in a different number of screen pixels, or, in common lingo, a different *monitor resolution.* Standard monitor resolution settings include 640 x 480 pixels, 800 x 600 pixels, 1024 x 768 pixels, and 1280 x 1024 pixels. The first number always indicates the number of horizontal pixels.

To size a screen picture, you simply match the pixel dimensions of the photo to the amount of screen real estate that you want the picture to consume. If your photo is 640 x 480 pixels, for example, it consumes the entire screen when the monitor resolution is set to 640 x 480. Raise the monitor resolution, and the same photo no longer fills the screen.

For a clearer idea of how monitor resolution affects the size at which your photo appears on the screen, see Figures 7-2 and 7-3. Both examples show a 640 x 480-pixel digital photo as it appears on a 17-inch monitor. (I used the Windows Desktop Properties control to display the photo as my Windows desktop background.) In Figure 7-2, I set the monitor resolution to 640 x 480. The image fills the entire screen (although the Windows taskbar hides a portion of the image at the bottom of the frame). In Figure 7-3, I displayed the same picture but switched the monitor resolution to 1280 x 1024. The image now eats up about one-fourth of the screen.

Figure 7-2: A 640 x 480-pixel digital photo fills the screen when the monitor resolution is set to 640 x 480.

Unfortunately, you often don't have any way to know or control what monitor resolution will be in force when your audience views your pictures. Someone viewing your Web page in one part of the world may be working on a 21-inch monitor set at a resolution of 1280 x 1024, while another someone may be working on a 13-inch monitor set at a resolution of 640 x 480. So you just have to strike some sort of compromise.

For Web images, I recommend sizing your photos assuming a 640 x 480 monitor resolution — the least common denominator, if you will. If you create an image larger than 640 x 480, people who use a monitor resolution of 640 x 480 have to scroll the display back and forth to see the entire photo. Of course, if you're preparing images for a multimedia presentation and you know what monitor resolution you'll be using, work with that display in mind.

Figure 7-3: At a monitor resolution of 1280 x 1024, a 640 x 480-pixel photo consumes roughly one-quarter of the screen.

Sizing images for the screen

To resize your image for screen display, follow the same procedures you use to size images for print, but choose pixels as your unit of measurement. The exact steps vary depending on your photo editor.

Remember to save a backup copy of your picture. In all likelihood, you're going to trim pixels from your photo for on-screen display. You may want those original pixels back someday, so save a copy of the picture under a different name before you go any farther.

If you increase the width or height value in your photo-editing software, you're adding pixels. The software has to make up — *interpolate* — the new pixels, and your picture quality can suffer. Check out the information on resampling and resolution in Chapter 2 for more details on this subject.

Also, the more pixels you have, the larger the image file. If you're preparing photos for the Web, file size is a special consideration because larger files take longer to download than smaller files. See "Nothing but Net: Photos on the Web" for more information about preparing images for use on Web pages.

Your photo editor should have an option to view your photo at the size it will display on-screen. Keep in mind that this view setting displays the photo according to your current monitor resolution; if displayed on a monitor using a different resolution, the photo size will change. For more on this sticky bit of business, refer to the preceding section.

Sizing screen images in inches

Newcomers to digital photography often have trouble sizing images in terms of pixels and prefer to rely on inches as the unit of measurement. And some photo-editing programs don't offer pixels as a unit of measurement in their image-size dialogue boxes.

If you can't resize your picture using pixels as the unit of measurement, or you prefer to work in inches, set the image width and height as usual and then set the output resolution to somewhere between 72 and 96 ppi.

Where does this 72 to 96 ppi figure come from? It's based on default monitor resolution settings on Macintosh and PC monitors. Mac monitors usually leave the factory with a monitor resolution that results in about 72 screen pixels per linear inch of the viewable area of the screen. PC monitors are set to a resolution that results in about 96 pixels for each linear inch of screen. So if you have a 1 x 1-inch picture and set the output resolution to 72 ppi, for example, you wind up with enough pixels to fill an area that's one-inch square on a Macintosh monitor.

Note that this approach is pretty unreliable because of the wide range of monitor sizes and available monitor resolution settings — the latter of which the user can change at any time, thereby blowing the 72/96 ppi guideline out of the water. For more precise on-screen sizing, the method described in the preceding section is the way to go.

Nothing but Net: Photos on the Web

If your company operates a World Wide Web site or you maintain a personal Web site, you can easily place pictures from your digital camera onto your Web pages.

Because I don't know which Web-page creation program you're using, I can't give you specifics on the commands and tools you use to add photos to your pages. But I can offer some advice on a general artistic and technical level, which is just what happens in the next few sections.

Basic rules for Web pictures

If you want your Web site to be one that people love to visit, take care when adding photos (and other graphics, for that matter). Too many images or images that are too big quickly turn off viewers, especially impatient viewers with slow modems. Every second that people have to wait for a picture to download brings them a second closer to giving up and moving on from your site.

To make sure that you attract, not irritate, visitors to your Web site, follow these ground rules:

✔ For business Web sites, make sure that every image you add is *necessary.* Don't junk up your page with lots of pretty pictures that do nothing to convey the message of your Web page — in other words, images that are pure decoration. These kinds of images waste the viewer's time and cause people to click away from your site in frustration.

✔ If you use a picture as a hyperlink — that is, if people can click the image to travel to another part of the site — also provide a text-based link. Why? Because many people (including me) set their browsers so that images are not automatically downloaded. Images appear as tiny icons that the viewer can click to display the entire image. It's not that I'm not interested in seeing important images — it's just that so many pages are littered with irrelevant pictures. When I use the Internet, I'm typically seeking information, not just cruising around looking at pretty pages. And I don't have time to download a bunch of meaningless images.

If you want to appeal to antsy folks like me, as well as to anyone who has a limited amount of time for Web browsing, set up your page so that people can navigate your site without downloading images if they prefer. My favourite sites are those that provide descriptive text with the image icon — for example, "Product shot" next to a picture of a manufacturer's hot new toy. This kind of labelling helps me decide which pictures I want to download and which ones will be of no help to me. At the very least, I expect navigational links to be available as text-based links somewhere on the page.

✔ Save your photos in either the JPEG or GIF file format. These formats are the only ones widely supported by different Web browsers. Two other formats, PNG (pronounced *ping*) and JPEG 2000, are in development, but not fully supported by either browsers or Web-page creation programs yet. You can read more about JPEG and GIF in the next three sections and more about file formats in general in Chapter 6.

✔ Strive for a total page download time of under a minute, using the lowest modem speed commonly in use today — 28.8 Kbps per minute — as your guideline. Sure, some lucky Web surfers have lightning-fast Internet connections, but most ordinary folks don't. The more pictures on a page, the smaller per-picture file size you need.

✔ Set the display size of your photos following the guidelines discussed in "Sizing images for the screen," earlier in this chapter. To accommodate the widest range of viewers, size your images with respect to a screen display of 640 x 480 pixels.

Remember, too, that the file size is determined by the total number of pixels in the image, not the output resolution. A 640 x 480-pixel image consumes as much disk space at 72 ppi as it does at 300 ppi. Check out Chapter 2 for a more detailed explanation of all this file-size, pixel-count, and output-resolution stuff.

✔ In addition to dumping pixels to get a smaller file size and reduce download times, you can compress the image using JPEG compression. Another alternative, although not always a good one, is to save the picture in the GIF format, which reduces the image to 256 colours, resulting in a smaller file size than a full-colour photo requires. The next section explains these options.

✔ Finally, a word of caution: Anyone who visits your page can download, save, edit, print, and distribute your image. So if you want to control the use of your picture, think twice about posting it on a Web page. You can also investigate digital watermarking and copyright protection services, which aim to prevent unauthorized use of your pictures. To start learning about such products, visit the Web site of one of the leading providers, Digimarc (www.digimarc.com). The Web site operated by the organization Professional Photographers of Canada (www.ppoc.ca) provides good background information on copyright issues in general.

Decisions, decisions: JPEG or GIF?

As discussed in the preceding section, JPEG and GIF are the two mainstream formats for saving photos that you want to put on a Web page. Both formats have their advantages and drawbacks.

✔ **Colour concerns:** JPEG *supports* 24-bit colour, which is the technical way of saying that images can contain approximately 16.7 million colours — full-colour photos, in plain English. GIF, on the other hand, can save only 8-bit images, which restricts you to a maximum of 256 colours.

For a better idea of the GIF format's colour limitation, in a colour image of a bowl of fruit — bananas, limes, and apples — the yellowish-green objects will be the bananas, the big green blobs will be the limes, and the red things will be the apples (unless you prefer Granny Smiths, which may make it difficult to distinguish between your limes and your apples).

The colour loss would be most noticeable in the bananas. In a 24-bit JPEG image, the subtle colour changes in bananas are realistically represented. But when the colour palette is limited to 256 colours, the range of available yellow shades is seriously reduced, so one shade of yellow must represent many similar shades. The resulting bananas will have a blotchy, unappetizing appearance.

For this reason, JPEG is better than GIF for saving *continuous-tone* images — images like photographs, in which the colour changes from pixel to pixel are very subtle. GIF is best reserved for greyscale images, which have only 256 colours or fewer to begin with, and for non-photographic images, such as line art and solid-colour graphics.

✔ **File size and compression:** With more colour information to store, a JPEG version of an image usually is much larger than a GIF version. Both JPEG and GIF enable you to compress image data in order to reduce file size, but JPEG uses *lossy* compression, while GIF uses *lossless* compression. (In most programs, GIF compression is applied automatically, without any input from you.)

Lossy compression dumps some image data, resulting in a loss of picture detail. Lossless compression, on the other hand, eliminates only redundant data so that any change in image quality is virtually undetectable. So although you can reduce a JPEG file to the same size as a GIF file, doing so typically requires a high degree of lossy compression, which can damage your image just as much as converting it from a 24-bit image to a 256-colour GIF file.

For more about various compression amounts, check out the section on compression settings in Chapter 5.

✔ **Web effects:** GIF offers two additional features that JPEG does not. First, you can produce *animated* GIF images, which are a series of pictures packaged into one file. When displayed on the Web, the images are flashed on and off in sequence to create the appearance of motion.

Second, you can make a portion of your image transparent, allowing the underlying Web-page background to show through. You can "fake" transparency with JPEG images if you're working with a plain Web page background, however. See "JPEG: The photographer's friend" for details.

Choosing between JPEG and GIF sometimes becomes a question of the lesser of two evils. Experiment with both formats to find out which one gives you the best-looking picture at the file size you need. In some cases, you may discover that shifting the image to 256 colours really doesn't have that much of an impact — if your photo has large expanses of flat colour, for example. Similarly, you may not notice a huge loss of quality on some pictures even when applying the maximum amount of JPEG compression, while other images may look like garbage with the same compression.

Many photo-editing programs offer a so-called *Web optimization* utility that assists you in making the call between JPEG and GIF. In addition to giving you a preview of how the photo will look if you use the various colour and compression settings available for GIF and JPEG, such utilities usually tell you how long the picture file will take to download at a particular modem speed. Again, be sure to select 28.8 Kpbs as your modem speed when checking the download time.

Would you like that picture all at once, or bit by bit?

Both JPEG and GIF enable you to specify whether your Web photos display gradually or all at once. If you create an *interlaced* GIF or *progressive* JPEG image, a faint representation of your image appears as soon as the initial image data makes its way through the viewer's modem. As more and more image data is received, the picture details are filled in bit by bit. With *noninterlaced* or *nonprogressive* images, no part of your image appears until all image data is received.

As with most things in life, this option involves a trade-off. Interlaced/progressive images create the *perception* that the image is being loaded faster

because the viewer has something to look at sooner. This type of photo also enables Web-site visitors to decide more quickly whether the image is of interest to them and, if not, to move on before the image download is complete.

However, interlaced and progressive images take longer to download fully, and some Web browsers don't handle these file options well. In addition, progressive JPEGs require more RAM (system memory) to view, and interlacing adds to the size of a GIF file. For all these reasons, most Web design experts recommend that you don't use interlaced or progressive images on your Web pages.

GIF: 256 colours or bust

The GIF format can support only 8-bit (256-colour) images. This colour limitation results in small file sizes that make for shorter download times, but it can also make your images look a little pixel-y and rough.

However, the quality loss that results from converting to 256 colours may not be too noticeable with some images. And, GIF does offer a feature that enables you to make a portion of your image transparent and to bundle a series of images into an animated GIF file.

GIF comes in two flavours: 87a and 89a. My, those are user-friendly names, aren't they? Anyway, 89a is the one that enables you to create a partially transparent image. With 87a, all your pixels are fully opaque. (Don't worry about remembering the numeric labels, though; most people just refer to the two types as *transparent GIF* and *non-transparent GIF.*)

Why would you want to make a portion of your image transparent? Well, suppose that you're selling estate jewellery on the Web. You have a photo of a new pin and earrings that you want to put on your site. The jewellery was shot against a black velvet background. If you save the image as a regular GIF image, viewers see both jewellery and velvet, as in the left example in Figure 7-4. If you make the velvet portions of the photo transparent, only the jewellery shows up on the Web page, as in the right example. The Web page background shows through the transparent velvet pixels.

Neither approach is right or wrong; GIF transparency just gives you an additional creative option. Note, too, that making some of your image pixels transparent doesn't reduce the size of the image file — the pixels are still in the file, they're just clear.

Saving a non-transparent GIF

If you use photo software that supports the GIF format, you should find the process of saving a non-transparent GIF to be pretty straightforward. But check your help system or manual just to be sure.

Some programs create and save a duplicate of your original image in the GIF format. But other programs instead overwrite the original image file. For safety's sake, always save a backup

Figure 7-4: Here you see the same photo as it appears on a Web page when saved as a standard GIF (left) and with GIF transparency enabled (right).

copy of your original image before you go forward. Remember that saving your image as a GIF file reduces the image to 256 colours, and you may want those original image colours back some day. In addition, saving the photo in the GIF format flattens your image — that is, merges all independent image layers into one. (See Chapter 9 for an explanation of image layers.)

At some point while saving a non-transparent GIF, your photo-editing software is likely to ask you to select (or de-select) a few GIF options. These options will probably have incredibly technical names, such as the ones listed in the following list, but they're not as complicated as they sound. The following options are presented in Adobe Photoshop Elements; if you're using different software, the options are likely to be similarly named.

✔ **Color Reduction Algorithm:** This option tells the program how to figure out which original image colours to keep when reducing the picture to 256 colours. In most cases, an option such as Adaptive works best, but try each one to see which does the least damage to your picture. As you change the option, the preview pane should automatically update the image.

If you want the program to give preference to the colours found in a certain area of the photo, select that area and then choose an option such as Selective as the Color Reduction Algorithm setting.

✓ **Dithering Algorithm:** When displaying a photo colour that's outside the limited 256-colour palette, the computer attempts to come close to the original colour by mixing colours that *are* found in the palette. Tech heads refer to this process as *dithering*.

The Dithering Algorithm option controls how Elements approaches, er, dithering. Don't give it another thought — just pick Diffusion for the best results in most cases. If you don't like how the preview looks with Diffusion, try one of the other methods to see whether the picture improves. I'm pretty sure it won't, but there's no harm in your trying.

✓ **Interlaced:** Leave this option turned off. To find out what it does, see the sidebar "Would you like that picture all at once, or bit by bit?"

✓ **Colors:** A GIF image can have a maximum of 256 colours. If you want to use all 256, set the Colors option to that number. But with some images that contain a small spectrum of colours, you may be able to get away with fewer colours, which reduces the image file size. Try lowering the Colors value and watch the right image preview to see how low you can go before the photo starts to fall apart.

✓ **Dither:** This setting adjusts how much dithering the program does when processing your photo. For the best possible results, leave the value at 100. However, lowering the value reduces file size, so again, you can try a lower setting and see whether the picture quality goes too far south.

Saving a GIF image with transparency

As with saving a standard GIF, you can take different avenues to wind up with a GIF image that contains transparent areas. In some programs, for example, you can make all pixels of a certain colour transparent during the file-saving process.

Depending on the program, you may be limited to making just one colour transparent, however. In addition, you typically have to make all pixels of the selected colour transparent, when you may want only pixels in the photo background to disappear.

When I'm working in Elements or Photoshop, I use a different and, I think, more flexible and reliable approach. Before saving the file, I just erase or delete any areas that I want to be transparent. That way, I control exactly which portions of the photo are invisible.

If your photo software doesn't let you have transparent pixels on the original background layer of an image, the workaround is to convert that background layer into a regular old image layer, which *can* have as many transparent pixels as you want. (Chapter 9 explains layers in detail, if you're unfamiliar with the concept.)

Of course, you should save a copy of your image file before you begin erasing, in case you ever want those pixels at full opacity in the future. Also note that if you want to use this technique on an existing GIF image, you must first convert the photo back to a full-colour photo.

When you finish creating your transparent areas and your photo is ready for the GIF factory, follow the same steps required by your software to save a non-transparent GIF, except for any matte and transparency options. The following options relate to Photoshop Elements:

- ✔ **Transparency:** This option controls whether your transparent pixels stay transparent or are filled with a solid
  colour when the file is saved. To keep your see-through
  pixels invisible, turn the option on. If you turn the option
  off, the program fills transparent areas with a solid colour,
  which you select from the Matte menu, explained next.

- ✔ **Matte:** This option enables you to select the solid colour
  that the program uses when you choose to fill transparent
  areas. It also affects your photo when the Transparency
  option is turned on.

  If you created your transparent areas in such a way that
  pixels around the edges are only partially transparent —
  for example, if you erased with a soft-edged brush — the
  program fills those partially clear pixels with the matte
  colour. Without this option, you can wind up with jagged

edges and a halo of background pixels around your subject. That's because when you don't apply a matte, pixels that are 50 percent or less transparent become fully opaque. Only pixels that are more than 50 percent transparent become completely clear.

I saved the image in Figure 7-5 with and without the matte feature. I used a soft-edged brush to erase the entire background before saving the file. In the left image in Figure 7-5, which I saved without taking advantage of the Matte option, you can see some stray black background pixels around the edges of the pitcher, and the edges also have a ragged look. In the right image, I applied a matte, matching the matte colour to the Web page background, which helps the edges of the pitcher look smoother and blend more gradually into the background.

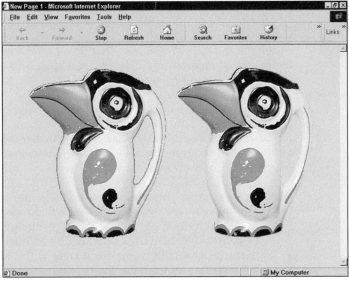

Figure 7-5: To avoid jagged edges and stray background pixels (left), set the Matte colour to match the Web page background (right).

JPEG: The photographer's friend

JPEG, which can save 24-bit images (16.7 million colours), is the format of choice for the best representation of continuous-tone images, including photographs. For more on the advantages and drawbacks of JPEG, see "Decisions, decisions: JPEG or GIF?" a few sections ago.

In order to create smaller files, however, JPEG applies lossy compression, which dumps some image data. Before you save an image in the JPEG format, be sure to save a backup copy using a file format that doesn't use lossy compression — TIFF, for example, or the Photoshop Elements format (PSD). After you apply JPEG compression, you can't get back the image data that gets eliminated during the compression process.

For more about compression, see Chapter 5. Note that JPEG also can't retain individual image layers, a feature explained in detail in Chapter 9.

When saving your images in the JPEG format for the Web, some photo editors, such as Adobe Photoshop Elements, enable you to find out how much damage your picture will suffer at various levels of JPEG compression. Check with your software's help system for the exact commands to use to save to JPEG.

When choosing the amount of compression to use, you're also determining the image quality and file size. The higher the quality, the less compression is applied, and the larger the file size.

If your software offers you a choice to create progressive or optimized JPEG files, you probably should kindly refuse the offer. For reasons discussed in the earlier sidebar, "Would you like that picture all at once, or bit by bit?," progressive JPEG files aren't usually a good idea. Optimized files are supposed to give you better image quality at a given compression setting, but they can cause problems with some Web browsers, so I recommend that you elect not to take advantage of the feature.

If the picture that you're saving contains transparent areas, you'll have to choose a matte colour. The transparent areas of your picture are always filled with a matte colour — white, if you don't select another colour. JPEG, as explained earlier in this chapter, can't deal with transparent pixels and so insists that you give them some colour.

If you're placing the photo on a Web page that has a solid-coloured background, you can make the transparent parts of a JPEG photo *appear* to retain their transparency, however. Just match the matte colour to the colour of your Web page background. The viewer's eye then won't be able to tell where the image stops and the Web page begins.

Drop Me a Picture Sometime, Won't You?

Having the ability to send digital photographs to friends and family around the world via e-mail is one of the most enjoyable aspects of owning a digital camera. With a few clicks of your mouse, you can send an image to anyone who has an e-mail account. That person can then view the photo on-screen, save it to disk, and even edit and print it.

Of course, this capability comes in handy for business purposes as well. As a part-time antiques dealer, for example, I often exchange images with other dealers and antiques enthusiasts around the country. When I need help identifying or pricing a recent find, I e-mail my contacts and get their feedback. Someone in the group usually can provide the information I'm seeking.

Although attaching a digital photo to an e-mail message is generally pretty simple, the process can sometimes break down due to differences in e-mail programs and how files are handled on the Mac versus the PC. Also, newcomers to the world of electronic mail often get confused about how to view and send images — which isn't surprising, given that e-mail software often makes the process less than intuitive.

One way to help make sure that your image arrives intact is to prepare it properly before sending. First, size your image according to the guidelines discussed earlier in this chapter, in "That's About the Size of It."

Also, save your image in the JPEG format. Some e-mail programs can accept GIF images, but not all can, so use JPEG for safety's sake. The exception is when sending images to CompuServe users, whose browsers sometimes work with GIF but not JPEG. (In other words, if the recipient has trouble with the image in one format, try resending the picture in the other format.)

Note that these instructions don't apply to pictures that you're sending to someone who needs the image for some professional graphics purpose — for example, if you created an image for a client who plans to put it in a company newsletter. In that case, save the image file in whatever format the client needs, and use the output resolution appropriate for the final output, as explained in Chapter 2. With large image files, expect long download times. As a matter of fact, unless you're on a tight deadline, putting the image on a Zip disk, CD, or some other removable storage medium and sending it off via overnight mail may be a better option than e-mail transmission.

That said, the following steps explain how to attach an image file to an e-mail message in Netscape Communicator in Version 4.0 of that program. If you're using a later version or some other e-mail program, the process is probably very similar, but check your program's online help system for specific instructions.

1. **Connect to the Internet and fire up Communicator.**

2. **Choose Communicator⇨Messenger (or click the little mail icon at the bottom of the program window).**

3. **Choose File⇨New⇨Message or click the New Msg button on the toolbar.**

   You're presented with a blank mail window.

4. **Enter the recipient's name, e-mail address, and subject information as you normally do.**

5. **Choose File⇨Attach⇨File or click the Attach button on the toolbar and then select File from the drop-down menu.**

   Most programs provide such a toolbar button — look for a button that has a paper clip icon on it. The paper clip has become the standard icon to represent the attachment feature.

   After you select the File option, you see a dialogue box that looks much like the one you normally use to locate and open a file. Track down the image file that you want to attach, select it, and click Open. You're then returned to the message composition window.

6. **Choose File⇨Send Now or click the Send toolbar button to launch that image into cyberspace.**

If everything goes right, your e-mail recipient should receive the image in no time. In Netscape Navigator, the image either appears as an *inline graphic* — that is, it is displayed right in the e-mail window as in Figure 7-6 — or as a text link that the user clicks to display the image.

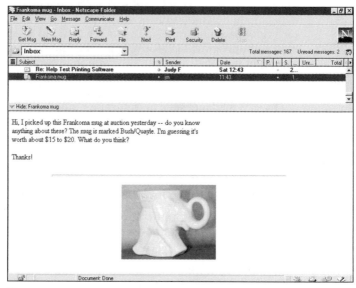

Figure 7-6: You can attach images to e-mail messages as shown here.

But as mentioned earlier, several technical issues can throw a monkey wrench into the process. If the image doesn't arrive as expected or can't be viewed, the first thing to do is call the tech support line for the recipient's e-mail program or service. Find out whether you need to follow any special procedures when sending images and verify that the recipient's software is set up correctly. If everything seems okay on that end, contact your own e-mail provider or software tech support. Chances are, some e-mail setting needs to be tweaked, and the tech support personnel should be able to help you resolve the problem quickly.

Part IV
Tricks of the Digital Trade

The 5th Wave   By Rich Tennant

"I'VE GOT SOME IMAGE EDITING SOFTWARE, SO I TOOK THE LIBERTY OF ERASING SOME OF THE SMUDGES THAT KEPT SHOWING UP AROUND THE CLOUDS. NO NEED TO THANK ME."

In this part...

If you watch many spy movies, you may have noticed that image editing has worked its way into just about every plot line lately. Typically, the story goes like this: A Mel Gibson-type hero snags a photograph of the bad guys. But the photograph is taken from too far away to clearly identify the villains. So Mel takes the picture to a buddy who works as a digital imaging specialist in a top-secret government lab. Miraculously, the buddy is able to enhance the picture enough to give Mel a crystal-clear image of his prey, and soon all is well for Earth's citizens. Except for the buddy, that is, who invariably gets killed by the villains just moments after Mel leaves the lab.

I'm sorry to say that, in real life, image editing doesn't work that way. Maybe top-secret government-types have software that can perform the tricks you see in movies — hey, for all I know, our agents really have ray guns and secret decoder rings, too. But the image editors available to you and me simply can't create photographic details out of nothing.

That doesn't mean that you can't perform some pretty amazing feats, though, as this part of the book illustrates. Chapter 8 shows you how to do minor touch-up work, such as cropping your image. Chapter 9 gives you a taste of some advanced editing techniques, such as painting on your image, creating photographic montages, and applying special-effects filters.

Although real-world image editing isn't nearly as dramatic as Hollywood implies, it's still way, way cool, not to mention a lot safer. Real-life image editors hardly ever get whacked by villains — although, if you doctor an image to show your boss or some other nemesis in an unflattering light, you may want to stay out of dimly lit alleys for a while.

Part IV

Tricks of the Digital Trade

The 5th Wave   By Rich Tennant

"I'VE GOT SOME IMAGE EDITING SOFTWARE, SO I TOOK THE LIBERTY OF ERASING SOME OF THE SMUDGES THAT KEPT SHOWING UP AROUND THE CLOUDS. NO NEED TO THANK ME."

In this part...

If you watch many spy movies, you may have noticed that image editing has worked its way into just about every plot line lately. Typically, the story goes like this: A Mel Gibson-type hero snags a photograph of the bad guys. But the photograph is taken from too far away to clearly identify the villains. So Mel takes the picture to a buddy who works as a digital imaging specialist in a top-secret government lab. Miraculously, the buddy is able to enhance the picture enough to give Mel a crystal-clear image of his prey, and soon all is well for Earth's citizens. Except for the buddy, that is, who invariably gets killed by the villains just moments after Mel leaves the lab.

I'm sorry to say that, in real life, image editing doesn't work that way. Maybe top-secret government-types have software that can perform the tricks you see in movies — hey, for all I know, our agents really have ray guns and secret decoder rings, too. But the image editors available to you and me simply can't create photographic details out of nothing.

That doesn't mean that you can't perform some pretty amazing feats, though, as this part of the book illustrates. Chapter 8 shows you how to do minor touch-up work, such as cropping your image. Chapter 9 gives you a taste of some advanced editing techniques, such as painting on your image, creating photographic montages, and applying special-effects filters.

Although real-world image editing isn't nearly as dramatic as Hollywood implies, it's still way, way cool, not to mention a lot safer. Real-life image editors hardly ever get whacked by villains — although, if you doctor an image to show your boss or some other nemesis in an unflattering light, you may want to stay out of dimly lit alleys for a while.

Chapter 8

Making Your Image Look Presentable

*O*ne of the great things about digital photography is that you're never limited to the image that comes out of the camera, as you are with traditional photography. With film, a lousy picture stays a lousy picture forever. Sure, you can get one of those little pens to cover up red-eye problems, and if you're really good with scissors, you can crop out unwanted portions of the picture. But that's about the extent of the corrections you can do without a full-blown film lab at your disposal.

With a digital image and a basic photo-editing program, however, you can do amazing things to your pictures with surprisingly little effort. In addition to cropping and adjusting brightness and contrast, you can cover up distracting background elements, bring back washed-out colours, paste two or more images together, and apply all sorts of special effects.

While Chapter 9 explores painting tools, special-effects filters, and other advanced photo-editing techniques, this chapter explains the basics: simple tricks you can use to correct minor defects in your pictures.

How to Open Your Photos

Before you can work on a digital photo, you have to open it inside your photo-editing program. In just about every program on the planet, you can use the following techniques to crack open a picture file:

- ✔ Choose File⇨Open.

- ✔ Use the universal keyboard shortcut for the Open command: Press Ctrl+O on a PC and ⌘+O on a Mac.

- ✔ Click the Open button on the toolbar. The universal symbol for this button is a file folder being opened.

Whichever method you choose, the program displays a dialogue box in which you can select the picture file that you want to open.

If you're working with the Windows version of Photoshop or Elements, you can zip to the file-opening dialogue box by double-clicking an empty area of the program window. Sorry, Mac users — this one doesn't work for you.

Here are a few other bits of gossip related to opening images:

- ✔ Some programs, including Elements, offer a built-in file browser that you can use to preview thumbnails of your picture files before you open them. You should be able to open a picture file by either double-clicking the thumbnail or dragging the thumbnail into the program window.

- ✔ Depending on your software, you may be able to open images directly from your camera (while the camera is connected to the computer). Check the program and camera manuals to find out how to make your software and hardware talk to each other. Look for information about something called a TWAIN driver. Chapter 6 provides additional enlightenment about this interesting acronym.

- ✔ Photo editing requires a substantial amount of free RAM (system memory). If your software balks when you try to open a picture, try shutting down all programs, restarting your computer, and then starting your photo software only. (Be sure to disable any start-up routines that launch programs automatically in the background when you fire up your system.) Now you're working with the maximum

RAM your system has available. If your computer continues to complain about a memory shortage, consider adding more memory — memory prices are relatively cheap right now, fortunately.

✔ Most programs need to use your computer's hard disk space as well as RAM when processing images. As a rule, you should have at least as much free disk space as you have RAM. If your system has 96MB of RAM, for example, you need 96MB of free disk space.

In Elements and Photoshop, you see a message saying that your *scratch disk* is full whenever you run out of the requisite amount of disk space. Other programs may use different terminology. In any case, you can solve the problem by deleting some unneeded files to free up some room on the hard disk.

✔ Most photo editors can't handle the proprietary file formats that some digital cameras use to store images. If your program refuses to open a file because of format, check your camera manual for information about the image-transfer software provided with your camera. You should be able to use the software to convert your images to a standard file format. (See Chapter 6 for a rundown of file formats.)

✔ If your picture opens up on its side, use your software's Rotate commands to set things right.

Save Now! Save Often!

Actually, a more appropriate name for this section would be "Saving Your Sanity." Unless you get in the habit of saving your images on a frequent basis, you can easily lose your mind.

Until you save your photo, all your work is vulnerable. If your system crashes, the power goes out, or some other cruel twist of fate occurs, everything you've done in the current editing session is lost forever. And don't think it can't happen to you because you popped for that state-of-the-art computer last month. Large digital images can choke even the most pumped-up system. I work on a souped-up computer with gobs of RAM, and I still get the occasional "This program has performed an illegal operation and will be shut down" message when working on large images.

To protect yourself, commit the following image-safety rules to memory:

- ✔ Stop, drop, and roll! Oops, no, that's fire safety, not image safety. Neither stopping, dropping, nor rolling will prevent your image from going up in digital flames should you ignore my advice on saving. Then again, when you tell your boss or client that you just lost a day's worth of edits, the stop-drop-roll manoeuvre is good for dodging heavy objects that may be hurled in your direction.

- ✔ To save a picture file for the first time, choose File⇨Save As. You're then presented with a dialogue box in which you can enter a name for the file and choose a storage location on disk, just as you do when saving any other type of document.

  If you don't want to overwrite your original photo file, be sure to give the picture a new name or store it in a separate folder from the original.

- ✔ While you're working on a picture, store it on your hard drive, rather than on a floppy disk or some other removable media. Your computer can work with files on your hard drive faster than files stored on removable media. But always save a backup copy on whatever removable storage media you use, too, to protect yourself in the event of a system crash. See Chapter 3 for information about different types of removable storage media.

- ✔ After you first save a picture, resave it after every few edits. You can usually simply press Ctrl+S (⌘+S on the Mac) to resave the image without messing with a dialogue box. Or click the Save button on the toolbar, which looks like a floppy disk.

- ✔ In most programs, you can specify which file format you want to use when you choose the Save As command. Always save photos-in-progress in your photo editor's *native format* — that is, the program's own file format — if one is available. In Elements and Photoshop, the native format is PSD.

  Why stick with the native format? Because it's designed to enable the program to process your edits more quickly. In addition, generic file formats, such as JPEG, GIF, and TIFF, may not be able to save some of the photo features, such as image layers. (Chapter 9 explains layers.)

Save your image in another format only when you're completely done editing. And before you save a file in JPEG or GIF, which destroy some picture data, be sure to save a backup copy of the original in a non-destructive format, such as TIFF. In most cases, your photo editor's native format should also be safe for making backups of original files.

Editing Safety Nets

As you make your way through the merry land of photo editing, you're bound to take a wrong turn every now and then. Perhaps you clicked when you should have dragged. Or cut when you meant to copy. Or painted a moustache on your boss's face when all you really intended to do was cover up a little blemish.

Fortunately, most mistakes can be easily undone by using the following options:

✔ The Undo command, usually found on the Edit menu, takes you one step back in time, undoing your last editing action. If you painted a line on your image, for example, Undo removes the line.

Undo can't bail you out of all messy situations, though. If you forget to save a picture file before you close it, you can't use Undo to restore all the work you did before closing. Nor can Undo reverse the Save command.

In many programs, you can choose Undo quickly by pressing Ctrl+Z on a PC or ⌘+Z on a Mac. The program toolbar may also offer Undo and Redo buttons.

✔ In most programs, you can choose the Print command without interfering with the option to use Undo. So you can make a change to your photo, print it, and then use Undo if you don't like the way the picture looks.

✔ Elements, Photoshop, and some other programs offer *multiple Undo,* which enables you to undo a whole series of edits rather than just one. Say that you crop your image, resize it, add some text, and then apply a border. Later, you decide that you don't want the text. You can go back to the point at which you added the text, and reverse your decision. Any edits applied after the one you undo are also eliminated, however. If you undo that text step, for example, the border step is also wiped out.

✔ If your image editor does not offer multiple Undo, choose Undo *immediately* after you perform the edit you want to reverse. If you use another tool or choose another command, you lose your opportunity to undo.

✔ Change your mind about that undo? Look for a Redo command (usually, the command is found on the Edit menu or in the same location as the Undo command). Redo puts things back to the way they were before you chose Undo.

As with Undo, some programs enable you to redo a whole series of Undo actions, while others can reverse only the most recent application of the Undo command. Check your software manual or help system to find out how much Undo/Redo flexibility you have. In Elements, use the Redo button or the Edit⇨Step Forward command to redo a batch of undone edits. You can also press Ctrl+Y (⌘+Y) repeatedly.

✔ File→Revert, found in Elements and Photoshop, restores your image to the way it appeared the last time you saved it. This command is helpful when you totally make a mess of your image and you just want to get back to square one. If your software doesn't offer this command, you can accomplish the same thing by simply closing your image without saving it and then reopening the image.

Cream of the Crop

Figure 8-1 shows a common photographic problem: great subject, lousy composition. In this example, my lovely nieces almost get lost in all that pool water. (The older one encouraged me to walk into the pool for a tighter shot, but somehow that didn't seem like a good idea, given that I was using an $800 camera that wasn't even mine!)

If this were a film photograph, I'd have to live with the results or find myself a sharp pair of scissors. But because this isn't a film photograph and because Photoshop Elements (and virtually every other photo editor) offers a Crop tool, I can simply clip away some of the pool, resulting in the much more pleasing image in Figure 8-2.

Figure 8-1: Suffering from an excess of boring background, this image begs for some cropping.

Figure 8-2: A tight cropping job restores emphasis to the subjects.

Most Crop tools in photo-editing programs work similarly. You pick up the Crop tool and drag to create a crop boundary around the area you want to keep. Drag from one corner of the area you want to keep to the other corner. The boundary appears on your image. Anything outside the boundary is earmarked for a trip to the digital dumpster. After you complete your drag, you see a little box at each corner of the crop boundary, and the area outside the crop boundary becomes shaded. You can drag the little boxes to adjust the crop outline if necessary. To move the entire boundary, drag anywhere inside the outline.

People who edit images for a living call those little boxes around the crop boundary *handles. Boxes* could be too easily understood by outsiders, you know.

If you don't like what you see after you apply the crop, use the Undo command to go back to square one.

A special function of the Crop tool in Elements, Photoshop, and some other programs enables you to rotate and crop an image in one fell swoop. Using this technique, you can straighten out images that look off-kilter, like the left image in Figure 8-3.

Figure 8-3: In some programs, you can crop and straighten an image in one step.

To take advantage of this feature in Elements, draw your crop boundary as described in the preceding steps. Then drag a corner crop handle up or down. A curved arrow cursor should appear near the handle, as shown in the left image in Figure 8-3. (The cursor appears above the top right handle in the figure.) After you click the Apply button, the program rotates and crops the image in one step. The right image in Figure 8-3 shows the results of my crop-and-rotate job.

Use this technique sparingly. Each time you rotate the image, the software reshuffles all the pixels to come up with the new image. If you rotate the same image area several times, you may begin to notice some image degradation.

Fixing Exposure and Contrast

At first glance, the underexposed picture on the left side of Figure 8-4 appears to be a throwaway. But don't give up on images like this, because with some creative editing, you may be able to rescue that too-dark image, as I did in the right image in Figure 8-4. This section explains how to use a variety of photo-editing tools to solve exposure problems.

Many photo-editing programs offer one-shot brightness/ contrast filters that adjust your image automatically. These automatic correction tools tend to do too much or too little and, depending on the image, can even alter image colours dramatically.

Figure 8-4: An underexposed image (left) sees new light, thanks to some brightness and contrast tweaking.

Fortunately, most programs also provide manual correction controls that enable you to specify the extent of the correction. These controls are very easy to use and almost always produce better results than the automatic variety.

The most basic exposure and contrast tools work by dragging a slider right or left to increase or decrease exposure or contrast. Or some programs enable you to enter values between 100 and –100 in a corresponding option box.

After you brighten an image, the colours may look a bit washed out. To bring some life back into your image, you may also need to tweak the contrast a bit. Drag the contrast slider right to increase contrast; drag left to decrease contrast.

Although the brightness/contrast filter is certainly easy to use, it's not always a terrific solution because it adjusts all colours in your picture by the same amount. That's fine for some pictures, but often, you don't need to make wholesale exposure changes.

For example, take a look at the butterfly photo on the left in Figure 8-5. The highlights are where they need to be, exposure-wise, as are the shadows. Only the midtones — areas of medium brightness — need lightening. In the right image in the figure, I raised the Brightness value enough to get the midtones to the right level. As you can see, this change amped up the highlights way too much. Pixels that were formerly light grey become white, and pixels that used to be black jump up the brightness scale, to dark grey. The overall result is a decrease in contrast and a loss of detail in the highlights and shadows.

When you're working with pictures that need selective exposure adjustments, you have a couple of options. If your photo editor offers a brightness/contrast filter only, you can select the area that you want to alter before applying the filter. That way, your changes affect the selected pixels only, and the rest of the photo remains the same.

If you're working with Elements, Photoshop, or some other advanced photo editor, you can use something called a *Levels filter,* with which you can adjust the shadows, midtones, and highlights in your image independently.

Figure 8-5: Raising the Brightness value enough to correct the midtones results in a loss of contrast and wipes out detail in the highlights and shadows.

Focus Adjustments (Sharpen and Blur)

Although no photo-editing software can make a terribly unfocused image appear completely sharp, you can usually improve things a bit by using a *sharpening filter*. A little sharpening can give extra definition to a slightly soft image.

When you're making this type of adjustment, be careful not to go overboard. Too much sharpening gives the picture a rough, grainy look. In addition, you can wind up with glowing colour halos along areas of high contrast. Also, even with the overabundance of sharpening, the blurrier portions of the background don't come into focus. You simply can't shift focus to this extent.

The following sections explain how to sharpen your image and also how to blur the background of an image, which has the effect of making the foreground subject appear more focused.

Sharpening 101

Before I show you how to sharpen your photos, I want to make sure that you understand what sharpening really does. Sharpening creates the *illusion* of sharper focus by adding small halos along the borders between light and dark areas of the image. The dark side of the border gets a dark halo, and the light side of the border gets a light halo.

To see what I mean, take a look at Figure 8-6. The top-left image shows four bands of colour before any sharpening is applied. Now look at the top-right image, which I sharpened slightly. Along the borders between each band of colour, you see a dark stripe on one side and a light stripe on the other. Those stripes are the sharpening halos.

Different sharpening filters apply the halos in different ways, creating different sharpening effects. The next few sections explain some of the common sharpening filters.

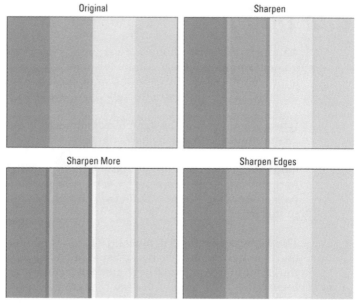

Figure 8-6: A close-up look at the effects of three sharpening filters available in Photoshop Elements.

Automatic sharpening filters

Sharpening tools, like other image-correction tools I discuss in this chapter, come in both automatic and manual flavours. With automatic sharpening filters, the program applies a pre-set amount of sharpening to the image.

Elements provides three automatic sharpening filters: Sharpen, Sharpen More, and Sharpen Edges. To try out the filters, choose Filter⇨Sharpen. Then click the name of the sharpening filter you want to apply. Your software may have automatic sharpening filters with similar names.

The following list explains how each of these automatic filters does its stuff. To see the filters in action, refer to Figure 8-6.

✔ The plain old Sharpen command sharpens your entire image. If your image isn't too bad off, Sharpen may do the trick. But more often than not, Sharpen doesn't sharpen the image enough.

✔ Sharpen More does the same thing as Sharpen, only more strenuously. I feel safe in saying that this command will rarely be the answer to your problems. In most cases, it simply oversharpens.

✔ Sharpen Edges looks for areas where significant colour changes occur — known as *edges* in digital imaging lingo — and adds the sharpening halos in those areas only. In Figure 8-6, for example, the sharpening halos appear between the two middle colour bars, where there is a significant change in contrast. But no halos are applied between those two bars and the outer bars. The intensity of the sharpening halos is the same as with Sharpen.

I suspect that Sharpen Edges won't do much for your images, either, but you can give it a try if you like. When you discover that I'm telling the truth, head for the Unsharp Mask filter, explained in the next section.

Depending on your software, you may find automatic sharpening filters similar to the ones just discussed. But the extent to which each filter alters your image varies from program to program, so do some experimenting. Again, for the best results, ignore the automatic sharpening filters altogether and rely on your program's manual sharpening controls, if available.

Manual sharpening adjustments

Some consumer-level photo-editing programs provide you with a fairly crude manual sharpening tool. You drag a slider one way to increase sharpening and drag in the other direction to decrease sharpening.

Elements, like Photoshop and other more advanced image-editing programs, provides you with the mother of all sharpening tools, which goes by the curious name of Unsharp Mask.

The Unsharp Mask filter is named after a focusing technique used in traditional film photography. In the darkroom, unsharp masking has something to do with merging a blurred film negative — hence, the *unsharp* portion of the name — with the original film positive in order to highlight the edges (areas of contrast) in an image. And if you can figure that one out, you're a sharper marble than I.

Despite its odd name, Unsharp Mask gives you the best of all sharpening worlds. You can sharpen your entire image or just the edges, and you get precise control over how much sharpening is done.

The Unsharp Mask dialogue box contains three sharpening controls: Amount, Radius, and Threshold. You find these same options in most Unsharp Mask dialogue boxes, although the option names may vary from program to program. Here's how to adjust the controls to apply just the right amount of sharpening:

✔ **Amount:** This value determines the intensity of the sharpening halos. Higher values mean more intense sharpening.

For best results, apply the Unsharp Mask filter with a low Amount value — between 50 and 100. If your image is too soft, reapply the filter using the same or lower Amount value. This technique usually gives you smoother results than applying the filter once with a high Amount value.

✔ **Radius:** The Radius value controls how many pixels neighbouring an edge are affected by the sharpening. With a small Radius value, the haloing effect is concentrated in a narrow region. If you set a higher Radius value, the halos spread across a wider area and fade out gradually from the edge.

Generally, stick with Radius values in the 0.5 to 2 range. Use values in the low end of that range for images that will be displayed on-screen; values at the high end work better for printed images.

✔ **Threshold:** This option tells the program how different two pixels must be before they're considered an edge and, thus, sharpened. By default, the value is 0, which means that the slightest difference between pixels results in a kiss from the sharpening fairy. As you raise the value, fewer pixels are affected; high-contrast areas are sharpened, while the rest of the image is not (just as when using Sharpen Edges, discussed in the preceding section).

When sharpening photos of people, experiment with Threshold settings in the 1 to 15 range, which can help keep the subject's skin looking smooth and natural. If your image suffers from graininess or noise, raising the Threshold value sharpens your image without making the noise even more apparent.

Blur to sharpen?

If your main subject is slightly out of focus and using the sharpening tools don't totally correct the problem, try this: Select everything but the main subject, using the techniques explained in the next chapter. Then apply a blur filter, found in most photo-editing programs, to the rest of the picture. Often, blurring the background in this way makes the foreground image appear sharper, as illustrated in Figure 8-7.

In this figure, I selected everything behind the car and applied a slight blur. I then reversed the selection so that the car and foreground were selected and applied just a wee bit of sharpening. As a result, the car not only looks much crisper than before, but the distracting background elements become much less intrusive on the main subject.

Figure 8-7: Applying a slight blur to everything behind the car makes the car appear more in focus and also helps de-emphasize the distracting background.

Chapter 9

Amazing Stuff Even You Can Do

. . . .

In This Chapter

▶ Painting on your digital photos

▶ Choosing your paint colours

▶ Filling a selected area with colour

▶ Replacing one colour with another

▶ Using layers for added flexibility and safety

▶ Erasing your way back to a transparent state

. . . .

*F*lip through any popular magazine, and you can see page after page of impressive digital art. A review of hot new computers features a photo in which lightning bolts are super-imposed over a souped-up system. A car ad shows a sky that's hot pink instead of boring old blue. A laundry detergent promotion has a backdrop that looks as though Van Gogh himself painted it. No longer can graphic designers get away with straightforward portraits and product shots — if you want to catch the fickle eye of today's consumer, you need something with a bit more spice.

Although some techniques used to create this kind of photographic art require high-end professional tools — not to mention plenty of time and training — many effects are surprisingly easy to create, even with basic photo software. This chapter gets you started on your creative journey by showing you a few simple tricks that can send your photographs into a whole new dimension. Use these ideas to make your marketing images more noticeable or just to have some fun exploring your creative side.

Give Your Image a Paint Job

Remember when you were in kindergarten and the teacher announced that it was time for finger painting? In a world that normally admonished you to be neat and clean, someone actually *encouraged* you to drag your hands through wet paint and make a colourful mess of yourself.

Photo-editing programs bring back the bliss of youth by enabling you to paint on your digital photographs. The process isn't nearly as messy as those childhood finger-painting sessions, but it's every bit as entertaining.

To paint in a photo editor, you can drag with your mouse or other pointing device to create strokes that mimic those produced by traditional art tools, such as a paintbrush, pencil, or airbrush. Or you can dump colour over a large area by selecting the area and then choosing the Fill command, which paints all selected pixels in one step.

Why would you want to paint on your photographs? Here are a few reasons that come to mind:

- ✔ You can change the colour of a particular object in your photo. Say that you shoot a picture of a green leaf to use as artwork on your Web site. You decide that you'd also like to have a red leaf and a yellow leaf, but you don't have time to wait for autumn to roll around so that you can photograph fall-coloured leaves. You can use your photo software to make two copies of the green leaf and then paint one copy red and the other yellow.

- ✔ You can hide minor flaws. Is a small blown highlight ruining an otherwise good photo? Set your paint tool to a colour matching the surrounding pixels, and dab the spot away.

  Paint tools also offer a way to get rid of red-eye — the demonic glint caused when a camera flash reflects in the subject's eyes. Choose a colour close to the natural eye colour, and paint over the red pixels.

- ✔ Aside from practical purposes, paint tools enable you to express your creativity. If you enjoy painting or drawing with traditional art tools, you'll be blown away by the possibilities presented by digital painting tools. You can blend photography and hand-painted artwork to create awesome images. I wish that I could show you some of my own artwork as an example of what I mean, but unfortunately I am absolutely talentless in this area, as evidenced by Figure 9-1. So I think it's better to send you to your local bookstore or library, where you can find all the creative inspiration and guidance you need in the many available volumes on digital painting.

Figure 9-1: A painted sun shines on a lakeside vista.

✔ And of course, painting tools provide you with one more way to adulterate photos of friends and family. Okay, you've probably already discovered this one on your own. Admit it, now — the first thing you tried in your photo software was painting a moustache on someone's picture, wasn't it?

Now that you know why you may want to pick up a paint tool, the following sections give you an introduction to some of the more common painting options. Put on your smock, grab a glass of milk and some graham crackers, and have a blast.

What's in your paint box?

Different photo editors offer different assortments of painting tools. Programs such as Corel Painter, geared toward photo artistry and digital painting, provide an almost unlimited supply of painting tools and effects. You can paint with brushes that mimic the look of chalk, watercolours, pastels, and even liquid metal. Figure 9-2 provides a sampling of different paint strokes you can create in this program.

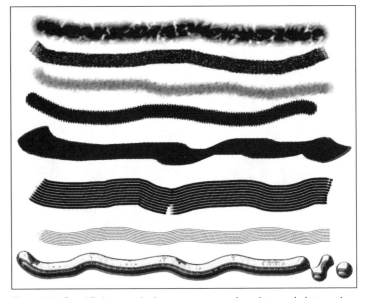

Figure 9-2: Corel Painter and other programs marketed toward photo artisans enable you to create a broad range of brush stroke effects.

If you're skilled at drawing or painting, you can express endless creative notions using this kind of program. You may also want to invest in a digital drawing tablet, which enables you to paint with a pen-like stylus, which most people find easier than using a mouse. (But be sure that the software you choose supports this function.)

Keep in mind that programs that emphasize painting tools sometimes don't offer as many image-correction or retouching options as programs such as Adobe Photoshop and Photoshop Elements, which concentrate on those functions rather than painting. On the other hand, programs that focus on retouching and correction usually don't offer a wide range of painting tools. Elements, for example, provides just a handful of painting tools.

Still, you can accomplish quite a bit even with a few basic painting tools. The following sections provide a brief introduction to the major Elements painting tools, which are similar to those found in most comparable programs.

Paintbrush, Airbrush, and Pencil

Your photo software likely provides at least three painting tools:

- ✔ **Paintbrush:** This tool typically can paint hard-edged strokes, like a ballpoint pen, or soft-edged strokes, like those painted with a traditional paintbrush.

- ✔ **Pencil:** A Pencil tool is usually limited to drawing hard-edged strokes.

- ✔ **Airbrush:** Digital airbrush tools create effects similar to what you can produce with a real-life airbrush. If you're never worked with one of those, imagine painting with spray paint.

In most versions of photo-editing software, you just drag across your image to lay down a paint stroke. Or click to put down a single spot of colour. When you work with the Airbrush, the tool pumps out more and more paint the longer you hold down the mouse button, even if you're not moving the mouse.

To paint a perfect horizontal or vertical stroke, press Shift as you drag. You can also paint a straight line by clicking at the spot where you want the line to begin and then Shift+clicking at the point where you want the line to end.

In Elements, as in most photo editors, you can adjust the following characteristics of the strokes that the paint tools produce:

- ✔ **Paint colour:** See the upcoming section "Pick a colour, any colour!" for information about this one.

- ✔ **Stroke size, softness, and shape:** You adjust these aspects of your paint strokes by choosing a different tool brush. In addition to changing the thickness and type of stroke edge — crisp or fuzzy — you can change the shape of the brush. You can paint with a square brush, for example, or even a brush that mimics calligraphic pen strokes.

✔ **Paint opacity:** You can make your paint strokes fully opaque, so that they completely obscure the pixels you paint over, or reduce the opacity so that some of the underlying image shows through the paint. Figure 9-3 shows examples of different opacity settings. I painted inside each of the letters with white but varied the opacity for each letter.

Figure 9-3: Change the paint opacity to create different effects.

✔ **Blending Mode:** A *blending mode* control enables you to mix your painted strokes with the underlying pixels in different ways. The upcoming section "Pouring colour into a selection" introduces you to a few blending modes.

For touch-up painting, the two most useful modes are Normal and Color. Use Normal when you want the painted pixels to cover the original pixels completely (assuming that the paint opacity is 100 percent). Color enables you to change the colour of an object realistically. The program applies the new colour to the pixels but uses the original brightness values. In other words, you retain the original highlights and shadows in the painted area. Try this mode when painting away red-eye pixels.

For greater painting flexibility, always paint on a new, independent image layer. That way, you can further adjust painted strokes after you create them by varying the opacity and blending mode of the layer itself. In addition, if you decide you don't like your painted pixels, you can get rid of them by simply deleting the layer. Read the section "Uncovering Layers of Possibility," later in this chapter, for the full story on layers.

Smudge tool

This tool, found in many photo editors, isn't so much a painting tool as a paint-smearing tool. It produces an effect similar to what you get when you drag your finger through a wet oil painting. When you drag with the Smudge tool, it takes whatever colour is underneath your cursor at the beginning of your drag and smears it over the pixels you touch over the course of your drag.

To get an idea of the kind of effects you can create with the Smudge tool, see Figure 9-4. I used the tool to give my antique pottery toucan a new 'do. Who says a toucan can't have a little fun, after all? To create the effect, I just dragged upward from the crown of the bird.

Figure 9-4: I used the Smudge tool to give my toucan a change of hairstyle.

In Elements, as in most other image-editing programs, you can adjust the Smudge tool brush and blending mode as you can for the painting tools, discussed in the preceding section. Also take note of these other Smudge options with Elements:

✔ **Finger Painting:** With this option, the Smudge tool smears the current foreground paint colour over your image instead of the colour that's under your cursor at the start of your drag. (See the next section to find out more about the foreground paint colour.)

✔ **Pressure or Strength:** This option adjusts the impact of the Smudge tool. At full strength, the Smudge tool smears the initial colour over the full length of your drag. At lower strengths, colour isn't smeared over the entire distance. I used a setting of about 70 percent when working on my toucan.

✔ **Use All Layers:** When you select this option, the Smudge tool smears colours from every visible image layer. This enables you to do your smudging on a layer separate from the rest of the photo. (See the section "Uncovering Layers of Possibility," later in this chapter, for more information about working with image layers.)

Pick a colour, any colour!

Before you lay down a coat of paint, you need to choose the paint colour. In most photo editors, two paint cans are available at any one time:

✔ **Foreground colour:** Usually, the major painting tools apply the foreground colour. In Elements, that includes the Paintbrush, Pencil, and Airbrush.

✔ **Background colour:** The background colour typically comes into play when you use certain special-effects filters that involve two colours. But in Elements, as in Photoshop, the Eraser tool also applies the background colour if you're working on the background layer of the photo. ("Uncovering Layers of Possibility," later in this chapter, provides details.) In addition, when you delete a selected area on the background layer, the resulting hole is filled with the background colour.

Check your software's online help system to figure out which tools paint in which colour — or just experiment by painting with each tool.

Like many other aspects of photo editing, the process of choosing the foreground and background colours is similar no matter what program you're using. Some programs provide a special colour palette in which you click the colour you want to use. Some programs rely on the Windows or Macintosh system colour pickers, while other programs, including Elements, provide you with a choice between the program colour picker and the system colour picker.

The next two sections explain how to choose a colour using the Windows system colour picker and the Macintosh colour picker. After you read about these colour pickers, you should have no trouble figuring out how to select colours in just about any program.

Using the Windows colour picker

Many Windows-based photo-editing programs enable you to choose colours using the Windows Color dialogue box, shown in Figure 9-5.

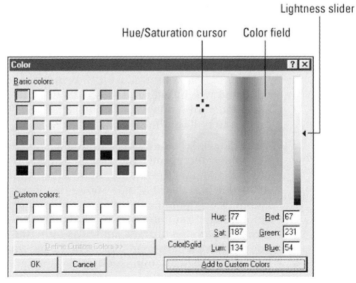

Figure 9-5: You can mix custom colours in the Windows system colour picker.

The following list explains how to use the dialogue box controls:

- ✔ To choose one of the colours in the Basic colors area, click its swatch.

- ✔ To access more colours, click the Define Custom Colors button at the bottom of the dialogue box. Clicking the button displays the right half of the dialogue box, as shown in Figure 9-5. (This button is greyed out in the figure because I already clicked it.)

- ✔ Drag the crosshair cursor in the colour field to choose the hue and saturation (intensity) of the colour, and drag the Lightness slider, to the right of the colour field, to adjust the amount of black and white in the colour.

- ✔ As you drag the cursor or the slider, the values in the Hue, Sat, and Lum boxes change to reflect the hue, saturation, and luminosity (brightness) of the colour. The Red, Green, and Blue option boxes reflect the amount of red, green, and blue light in the colour, according to the RGB colour model.

- ✔ After you produce a colour you like, you can add the colour to the Custom colors palette on the left side of the dialogue box by clicking the Add to Custom Colors button. The palette can hold up to 16 custom colours. To use one of the custom colours on your next trip to the dialogue box, click the colour's swatch.

- ✔ To replace one of the Custom colors swatches with another colour, click that swatch before clicking the Add to Custom Colors button. If all 16 swatches are already full, Windows replaces the selected swatch (the one that's surrounded by a heavy black outline). Click a different swatch to replace that swatch instead.

- ✔ The Color/Solid swatch beneath the colour field previews the colour. Technically, the swatch displays two versions of your colour — the left side shows the colour as you've defined it, and the right side shows the nearest solid colour. See, a monitor can display only so many solid colours. The rest it creates by combining the available solid colours — a process known as dithering. Dithered colours have a patterned look to them and don't look as sharp on-screen as solid colours.

How many solid colours are available to you depends on the settings of your system's video card. Today, most people set their systems to display at least 32,000 colours, also known as 16-bit colour. But people working on older computers may be limited to as few as 256 colours. For this reason, many Web designers limit their image colour palettes to 256 solid colours or fewer.

If you're creating Web images and want to stick with solid colours, set your monitor to display a maximum of 256 colours before heading to the Color dialogue box. Otherwise, you won't see any difference between the two sides of the Color/Solid swatch. After defining a colour, click the right side of the swatch to select the nearest solid colour.

After you choose your colour, click OK to leave the dialogue box.

Using the Apple colour picker

If you're working on a Macintosh computer, your photo software may enable you — or require you — to select colours using the Apple colour picker, shown in Figure 9-6.

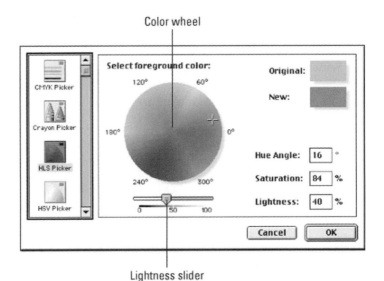

Color wheel

Lightness slider

Figure 9-6: In the Apple colour picker, you can blend colours by adjusting the hue, saturation, and lightness values.

The colour picker design varies slightly with different versions of the Mac operating system — the one shown in the figure is from Mac OS 9.1. But the basics remain the same. At the very least, the colour picker enables you to select a colour using either the Apple HSL colour model, which sometimes goes by the alternative name HLS, or the Apple RGB colour model.

Apple HSL (Hue, Saturation, and Lightness) is a variation of the standard HSB (Hue, Saturation, and Brightness) colour model.

Use whichever colour model suits your fancy — click the icons on the left side of the dialogue box to switch between the colour models. In HSL mode, drag the crosshair in the colour wheel to set the hue (colour) and saturation (intensity) of the colour, as shown in the figure. Drag the lightness slider bar to adjust the lightness of the colour. In RGB mode, drag the R, G, and B colour sliders to select your colour or enter values in the Red, Green, and Blue option boxes.

Whichever colour model you use, the Original and New boxes at the top of the dialogue box represent the current foreground or background colour and the new colour you're mixing, respectively. When you're satisfied with your colour, press Return or click OK.

Pouring colour into a selection

Brushing paint over a large area can be tedious, which is why most photo-editing programs provide a menu command that fills an entire selected area with colour. Most programs call this command the Fill command. However, the result of using the Fill command can be a look that's entirely unnatural because a normal fill pours solid colour throughout your selection, obliterating the shadows and highlights of the original photograph.

To enable you to create more natural-looking fills, many programs offer a choice of *blending modes,* which you can use to combine the fill pixels with the original pixels in slightly different ways. A Color blend mode, which is available in most programs that offer blending modes, applies the fill colour while retaining the shadows and highlights of the underlying image.

Programs that provide blending modes tend to offer the same assortment of modes. I could provide you with an in-depth description of how different blend modes work, but frankly, predicting how a blending mode will affect an image is difficult even if you have this background knowledge. So just play around with the available modes until you get an effect you like.

Your software may also offer two other fill options: You may be able to vary the opacity of the fill so that some of the underlying image pixels show through even with the Normal blending mode. And you may be able to fill the selection with a pattern instead of a solid colour. This last option is especially useful for creating backgrounds for collages.

I'm about to show you yet one more way to fill a portion of your image with colour. But before I do, I want to say that I don't recommend using this method. I bring it up here only because many programs offer this option, and new users invariably gravitate toward it.

The feature in question is a special tool that is a combination of a selection tool and a Fill command. Elements calls the tool the Paint Bucket; the tool's icon in the toolbox looks like a paint bucket, as does the tool cursor. (You can see the cursor in Figure 9-7.) In other programs, this tool is often called the *Fill tool,* but it usually works quite differently from the *Fill command* discussed earlier.

When you click in your image with the tool, the program selects an area of the image as though you had clicked with the Magic Wand (or whatever the colour selection tool is called in your software). If you click a red pixel, for example, red pixels are selected. Then the selected area is filled with the foreground colour.

So what's my problem with this tool? The results are too unpredictable. You can't tell in advance how much of your image will be filled. As an example, see Figure 9-7. The paint-bucket cursor indicates the spot I clicked; the white area is the resulting fill. Had I clicked just a few pixels to the left or right, a totally different region of the apple would have been painted white. For more accurate results, select the area you want to fill manually. Then use your regular Fill command or a painting tool to colour the selection.

Paint-bucket cursor

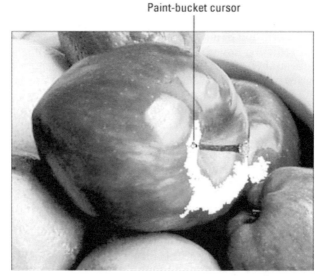

Figure 9-7: Clicking with the Paint Bucket fills similarly coloured pixels with the foreground colour (white, in this case).

Uncovering Layers of Possibility

Photoshop Elements, Photoshop, and many other photo-editing programs provide an extremely useful feature called *layers*. Layers sometimes go by other names, such as Objects, Sprites, or Lenses. But whatever the name, this feature is key to creating many artistic effects and is also extremely helpful for ordinary retouching work.

To understand how layers work, think of those clear sheets of acetate used to create transparencies for overhead projectors. Suppose that on the first sheet, you paint a birdhouse. On the next sheet, you draw a bird. And on the third sheet, you add some blue sky and some green grass. If you stack the sheets on top of each other, the bird, birdhouse, and scenic background appear as though they are all part of the same picture.

Layers work just like that. You place different elements of your image on different layers, and when you stack all the layers on top of each other, you see the *composite image* — the elements of all the layers merged together. Where one layer is empty, pixels from the underlying layer show through.

You gain several image-editing advantages from layers:

✔ You can shuffle the *stacking order* of layers to create different pictures from the same layers, as shown in Figure 9-8. (Stacking order is just a fancy way of referring to the arrangement of layers in your image.)

Both images contain three layers: one for the pond and trees, one for the lily, and one for a prehistoric-looking creature that I probably should be able to name but can't. The pond-and-trees scene occupies the bottom layer in both pictures. In the left image, I put the reptilian thing on the second layer and placed the lily on the top layer. Because the lily obscures most of the reptile layer, the picture appears to show nothing more menacing than a giant, mutant lily. Reversing the order of the top two layers reveals that what appeared to be the stem of the lily actually is the tail of a science experiment gone wrong.

To make the end of the tail appear to be immersed in the water, I dragged across the tail with my photo-editor's Eraser tool set to 50-percent opacity. You can read more about this technique in "Editing a multilayered image,"

Figure 9-8: What appears to be a peaceful, lily-in-a-pond scene (left) becomes far more sinister when the order of the top and middle image layers is reversed (right).

later in this chapter. I also painted subtle shadows, using a soft brush and a low opacity setting, under both the scaly thing and the lily to make the scene appear a bit more realistic.

✔ Layers also make experimenting easier. You can edit objects on one layer of your image without affecting the pixels on the other layers one whit. So you can apply the paint tools, retouching tools, and even image-correction tools to just one layer, leaving the rest of the image untouched. You can even delete an entire layer without repercussions.

Suppose that you decide you want to get rid of the lily in Figure 9-8 so that the scaly monster appears to walk on water. If the lily, reptile, and background all existed on the same layer, deleting the lily would leave a flower-shaped hole in the image. But because the three elements are on separate layers, you can simply delete the lily layer. In place of the jettisoned flower petals, the water from the background layer appears.

✔ Layers simplify the process of creating photo collages, too. By placing each element in the collage on a different layer, you can play around with the positioning of each element to your heart's content.

✔ You can vary the opacity of layers to create different effects. Figure 9-9 shows an example. Both images contain two layers: The rose is on the top layer, while the faded wood occupies the bottom layer. In the left image, I set the opacity of both layers to 100 percent. In the right image, I lowered the opacity of the rose layer to 50 percent so that the wood image is partially visible through the rose. The result is a ghostly rose that almost looks like part of the wood.

✔ You can vary how the colours in one layer merge with those in the underlying layers by applying different blending modes. Layer blending modes determine how the pixels in two layers are mixed together, just like the fill and paint blending modes discussed earlier in this chapter. Different blending modes, such as Normal and Color, create different fill effects. These same blending modes, as well as many others, are usually available for blending layers. Some blending modes create wacky, unearthly colour combinations, perfect for eye-catching special effects, while others, like Color, are useful for changing image colours with natural-looking results.

Figure 9-9: At left, the rose layer rests atop the wood layer at 100 percent opacity. At right, I set the rose layer opacity to 50 percent, turning the rose into a ghost of its former self.

> ✔ In some programs, you can apply an assortment of automatic layer effects. Elements, for example, provides an effect that adds a drop shadow to the layer. If you move the layer, the shadow moves with it.

Not all photo-editing programs provide all these layer options, and some entry-level programs don't provide layers at all. But if your program offers layers, I urge you to spend some time getting acquainted with this feature. I promise that you will never go back to unlayered editing after you do.

Layers do have one drawback, however: Each layer increases the file size of your image and forces your computer to expend more memory to process the image. So after you're happy with your image, you should smash all the layers together to reduce the file size — a process known as *flattening* or *merging,* in image-editing parlance.

After you merge layers, though, you can no longer manipulate or edit the individual layer elements without affecting the rest of the image. So if you think you may want to play around with the image more in the future, save a copy in a file format that supports layers. Check your software's help system for specifics on flattening and preserving layers.

If you want some more specifics on using layers, the next sections provide some basics about layer functions in Elements.

Although layer functions vary from program to program, the available features tend to be similar no matter what the program. So reading through what's available with Photoshop Elements should give you a head start on understanding your program's layering tools.

Working with Elements layers

To view, arrange, and otherwise manipulate image layers in Photoshop Elements, you need to display the Layers palette. To open the palette, click its tab in the palette well or choose View➪Show Layers.

Here's a quick tour of the Layers palette:

- Each layer in the image is listed in the palette. To the left of the layer name is a thumbnail view of the layer contents.

  By default, transparent areas appear as a checkerboard pattern. If you want to change that display, choose Edit➪ Preferences➪Transparency to open the Transparency panel of the Preferences dialogue box, where the transparency options are housed.

- Only one layer at a time is *active* — that is, available for editing. The active layer is highlighted in the Layers palette. To make a different layer active, click its name in the palette.

- The eyeball icon indicates whether the layer is visible in the image. Click the icon to hide the eyeball and the layer. Click in the now-empty eyeball column to redisplay the layer.

- Click the right-pointing arrow at the top of the palette to open the Layers palette menu, which contains layer-management commands. (In Elements 2.0, the arrow is on a button labeled *More.*) Most commands found on the palette menu also appear on the Layer menu at the top of the program window.

- You can choose two of the most-frequently used commands, New Layer and Delete Layer, by clicking the New Layer and Trash buttons at the bottom of the palette. For more on adding and deleting layers, pass your peepers over the next section.

✔ Click the Adjustment Layer button to create a special type of layer that enables you to apply colour and exposure changes without permanently altering the original image.

✔ The Blending Mode menu and Opacity control enable you to adjust the way that pixels on a layer blend with pixels on the layer below. These controls work just like the blending mode and opacity controls described earlier, in the discussion about the Fill command, except that the Layers palette controls affect pixels that already exist on a layer. The Fill command controls affect pixels that you're about to paint, as do the Mode and Opacity controls related to the painting tools.

✔ The Lock controls near the top of the palette enable you to "lock" the contents of a layer, thereby preventing you from messing up a layer after you get it just so. The leftmost of the two lock controls prevents you from making any changes to transparent parts of the layer; the right control prevents you from altering the entire layer. However, in either case, you can still move the layer up and down in the layer stack.

To preserve independent layers between editing sessions, you must save the image file in a format that *supports* layers — that is, can deal with the layers feature. In Elements, go with the program's native format, PSD. See Chapter 6 for more details about file formats and saving files.

Adding, deleting, and flattening layers

Every Elements image starts life with one layer, named *Background* layer. You can add and delete layers as follows:

✔ To add a new layer, click the New Layer button in the Layers palette. Your new layer appears directly above the layer that was active at the time you clicked the button. The new layer becomes the active layer automatically.

✔ To duplicate a layer, drag it to the New Layer button.

✔ To delete a layer — and everything on it — drag the layer name to the Trash button in the Layers palette. Or click the layer name and then click the Trash button.

✔ *Flattening* an image means to merge all independent image layers into one. Flattening an image has two benefits: First, it reduces the file size and the amount of muscle your computer needs to process your edits. Second, it prevents you from accidentally moving things out of place after you arrange them to your liking.

After you flatten the image, however, you can no longer manipulate the layers independently. So be sure that you're really satisfied with your picture before you take this step. You may want to make a backup copy of the picture in its multilayered state just for good measure.

To flatten your image, choose Layer⇨Flatten Image from either the Layers palette menu or the Layer menu at the top of the program window.

✔ In addition to flattening all layers, you can merge just two or more selected layers together. To go this route, you have a couple of options:

• To merge a layer with the layer immediately underneath, click the upper layer in the pair and then choose Merge Layers from either the palette menu or the main Layer menu. If your image has more than two layers, this command is called Merge Down.

• To merge two layers that aren't adjacent, or to merge more than two layers, first hide the layers that you don't want to fuse together. (Click their eyeball icons in the Layers palette.) Then choose Merge Visible from the palette menu or main Layer menu. After you merge the visible layers, redisplay the hidden layers.

Editing a multilayered image

Editing multilayered images involves a few differences from editing a single-layer image. Here's the scoop:

✔ **Changing layer order:** Drag a layer name up or down in the Layers palette to rearrange the layer's order in your image.

✔ **Selecting the entire layer:** To select an entire layer, just click its name in the Layers palette. For some commands, however, you must use the Select⇨Select All command to create a layer-wide selection outline. (If a command that you want to use appears dimmed in a menu, this is likely the cause.)

✔ **Selecting part of a layer:** Create a selection outline and then click the layer name in the Layers palette, if the layer isn't already the active layer.

A selection outline always affects the active layer, even if another layer was active when you created the outline.

✔ **Copy a selected area to a new layer:** Press Ctrl+J in Windows; press ⌘+J on a Mac. Or choose Layer⇨New⇨ Layer via Copy. Your selection goes on a new layer immediately above the layer that was active when you made the copy.

✔ **Deleting a selection:** On any layer but the background layer, deleting something creates a transparent hole in the layer, and the underlying pixels show through the hole. If you delete a selection on the background layer, the hole becomes filled with the current background colour.

✔ **Erasing on a layer:** On any layer but the background layer, you can also use the Eraser tool to rub a hole in a layer, as I did in Figure 9-10. In the left half of the image, I nestled my ceramic elf into a field of wildflowers, with the elf occupying the top layer in the image and the wildflowers consuming the bottom layer. The right half of the image shows me swiping away at the elf's chest and legs with the Eraser, bringing the wildflowers in the bottom layer into view.

As with the Elements painting tools, you can adjust the impact of the Eraser by changing the Opacity value on the Options bar. At 100 percent, you swipe the pixels clean; anything less than 100 percent leaves some of your pixels behind. I used a lowered Eraser opacity when creating the collage image in Figure 9-8, earlier in this chapter. Using a soft brush and 50 percent tool opacity, I erased the lower portion of the lizardy-thing's tail to make the tail appear to hang in the water.

✔ **Erasing on the background layer:** If you're working on the background (bottom) layer, using the Eraser doesn't result in a transparent area. Instead, the erased area is filled with the current background colour, just as when you delete something from the background layer.

Eraser cursor

Figure 9-10: After putting the elf on the top layer and the wildflowers on the bottom layer (left), I used the Eraser tool to rub away some elf pixels, revealing the underlying wildflower pixels (right).

What if you want areas of your background layer to be transparent — say, to create a single-layer GIF image with transparent areas? The trick is to convert the background layer to a "regular" layer. Click the background layer name in the Layers palette and then choose Layer⇨New⇨ Layer from Background.

Head to Chapter 7 for details about how to preserve the transparent areas when you save the picture in the GIF format. The same chapter shows you how to fill the transparent areas with colour when you save the file in the JPEG format.

✔ **Moving a layer:** Click the layer name in the Layers palette to select the layer. Then drag in the image window with the Move tool. Note that if the Auto Select Layer check box is selected on the Options bar, clicking any pixel on a layer automatically selects the layer that contains that pixel.

✔ **Transforming a layer:** After clicking the layer name in the Layers palette, use the commands on the Image menu to rotate, flip, and otherwise transform a layer. You can use the same techniques and commands as when you transform a selected area.

Remember that resizing and rotating image elements can damage your image quality. You can typically reduce your image without harm, but don't try to enlarge the image very much, and don't rotate the same layer repeatedly.

Also don't forget to save your image file in the native Elements file format, PSD, if you want to retain your individual image layers between editing sessions.

Part V
The Part of Tens

The 5th Wave   By Rich Tennant

In this part...

Some people say that instant gratification is wrong. I say, phooey. Why put off until tomorrow what you can enjoy this minute? Heck, if you listen to some scientists, we could all get flattened by a plunging comet or some other astral body any day now, and then what will you have for all your waiting? A big fat nothing, that's what.

In the spirit of instant gratification, this part of the book is designed for those folks who want information right away. The chapters herein present useful tips and ideas in small snippets that you can rush in and snag in seconds. Without further delay. *Now,* darn it. Chapter 10 offers ten techniques for creating better digital images; Chapter 11 gives you ten suggestions for ways to use your images.

If you like things quick and easy, this part of the book is for you. And if instant gratification is against your principles, you may want to . . . look up! I think that big, black ball in the sky is an asteroid, and it's headed this way!

Chapter 10

Ten Ways to Improve Your Digital Images

In This Chapter

▶ Capturing the right number of pixels

▶ Choosing the optimum compression setting

▶ Composing a scene for maximum impact

▶ Shedding some light on the subject

▶ Avoiding "shaky" images

▶ Acquiring a digital perspective

▶ Correcting flaws inside your photo software

▶ Choosing paper for the best printed output

▶ Spending quality time with your camera

▶ Paying attention to the manufacturer's instructions

*D*igital cameras have a high "wow" factor. That is, if you walk into a room full of people and start snapping pictures with your digital camera, just about everyone in the room will say, "Wow!" and ask for a closer look. Oh sure, one guy will look unimpressed and even make a few snide remarks, but that's just because he's secretly jealous that you managed to sneak up unnoticed and kick his keister in the who's-got-the-latest-and-greatest-technology game.

Sooner or later, though, people will stop being distracted by the whiz-bang technology of your camera and start paying attention to the quality of the pictures you turn out. And if your images are poor, whether in terms of image quality or photographic composition, the initial "wows" turn to "ews," as in "Ew, that picture's *terrible.* You'd think after spending all that money on a digital camera, you could come up with something better than *that.*"

So that you don't embarrass yourself — photographically speaking, anyway — this chapter presents ten ways to create better digital images. If you pay attention to these guidelines, your audience will be as captivated by your pictures as they are by your shiny digital camera.

Remember the Resolution!

When you print digital photos, the image output resolution — the number of pixels per linear inch — makes a big impact on picture quality. To get the best results from most printers, you need an output resolution of between 200 to 300 pixels per inch (ppi).

Most digital cameras offer a few different capture settings, each of which delivers a certain number of pixels. Before you take a picture, consider how large you may want to print the photo. Then select the capture setting that gives you the number of pixels you need to be able to print a good picture at that size.

Remember that you usually can get rid of excess pixels in your photo software without affecting picture quality, but you almost never get good results from adding pixels. In other words, better to wind up with too many pixels rather than too few.

Don't Overcompress Your Images

Most cameras enable you to select from several *compression* settings. Compression is a technique used to shrink the size of an image file. In most cases, camera compression settings have quality-related names — Best, Better, Good, for example, or Fine and Normal. That's appropriate because compression affects picture quality.

Digital cameras typically use *lossy* compression — meaning that some image data is sacrificed during the compression process. The more lossy compression you apply, the lower the photo quality. So for the best-looking images, shoot your pictures using the setting that applies the least amount of compression. Of course, less compression means larger file sizes, so you can't fit as many pictures in the camera's memory as you can at a lower-quality setting.

You also need to consider the compression factor when saving your images after editing them. Some file formats, such as JPEG, apply lossy compression during the save process, while others, such as TIFF, use *lossless* compression. With lossless compression, your file size isn't reduced as much as with lossy compression, but you don't lose important image data.

Look for the Unexpected Angle

Changing the angle from which you photograph your subject can add impact and interest to the picture. Instead of shooting a subject straight on, investigate the unexpected angle — lie on the floor and get a bug's-eye-view, for example, or perch yourself on a sturdy chair and capture the subject from above.

As you compose your scenes, also remember the rule of thirds — divide the frame into vertical and horizontal thirds and position the main focal point of the shot at a spot where the dividing lines intersect. And quickly scan the frame for any potentially distracting background elements before you press the shutter button.

Light 'Er Up!

When you're working with a digital camera, good lighting is essential for good pictures. The light sensitivity of most digital cameras is equivalent to the sensitivity of ISO 100 film, which means that shooting in low lighting usually results in dark and grainy images.

If your camera has a flash, you may need to use the flash not just when shooting in dimly lit interiors, but also to bring your subjects out of the shadows when shooting outdoors. For extra flash flexibility, you can buy accessory slave flash units that work in conjunction with your camera's built-in flash.

Some higher-end cameras also have a synchronization socket for connecting an extension flash. To shed even more light on the situation, you may want to invest in some inexpensive photography lights.

Use a Tripod

To capture the sharpest possible image, you must hold the camera absolutely still. The slightest movement can result in a blurry image.

This statement applies to shooting with film as well as when you use a digital camera, of course. But the exposure time required by the average digital camera is comparable to that required by ISO 100 film. If you're used to shooting with a film that's faster than ISO 100, remember that you need to hold your digital camera still for a slightly longer period of time than you do when taking film pictures.

For best results, use a tripod, especially when shooting in dimly lit settings.

Compose from a Digital Perspective

When you compose pictures, fill as much of the frame as possible with your subject. Try not to waste precious pixels on a background that will be cropped away in the editing process.

If you're shooting objects that you plan to use in a photo collage, set the objects against plain, contrasting backgrounds. That way, you can easily select the subject using photo-editing tools that select pixels according to colour (such as the Magic Wand in Photoshop Elements).

Take Advantage of Image-Correction Tools

Don't automatically toss photos that don't look as good as you would like. With some judicious use of your photo software's retouching tools, you can brighten up under-exposed images, crop out distracting background elements, and even cover up small blemishes.

Some of these basic techniques you can use to enhance your images are simple to use, requiring just one click of the mouse button. Others involve a bit more effort but are still easily mastered if you put in a little time.

Being able to edit your photographs is one of the major advantages of shooting with a digital camera. So take a few minutes each day to become acquainted with your photo software's correction commands, filters, and tools. After you start using them, you'll wonder how you got along without them.

Print Your Images on Good Paper

The type of paper you use when printing your images can have a dramatic effect on how your pictures look. The same picture that looks blurry, dark, and oversaturated when printed on cheap copy paper can look sharp, bright, and glorious when printed on special glossy photographic paper.

Check your printer's manual for information on the ideal paper to use with your model. Some printers are engineered to work with a specific brand of paper, but don't be afraid to experiment with paper from other manufacturers. Paper vendors are furiously developing new papers that are specifically designed for printing digital images on consumer-level colour printers, so you just may find something that works even better than the recommended paper.

Practise, Practise, Practise

Digital photography is no different from any other skill in that the more you do it, the better you become. So shoot as many pictures as you can, in as many different light situations as you can. As you shoot, jot down the camera settings you used and the lighting conditions at the time you snapped the image. Later, evaluate the pictures to see which settings worked the best in which situations.

If your camera stores the capture settings as metadata in the image file, you don't need to bother writing down settings for each shot. Instead, you can use a special piece of software to view the capture settings for each image that you download to your computer.

After you spend some time experimenting with your camera, you'll start to gain an instinctive feel for what tactics to use in different shooting scenarios, increasing the percentage of great pictures in your portfolio. As for those pictures that don't make the grade, keep them to yourself.

Read the Manual (Gasp!)

Remember that instruction manual that came with your camera? The one you promptly stuffed in a drawer without bothering to read? Go get it. Then sit down and spend an hour devouring every bit of information inside it.

I know, I know. Manuals are deadly boring. But you aren't going to get the best pictures out of your camera unless you understand how all its controls work. I can give you general recommendations and instructions in this book, but for camera-specific information, the best resource is the manufacturer's own manual.

After your initial read-through, drag the manual out every so often and take another pass at it. You'll probably discover the answer to some problem that's been plaguing your pictures or be reminded of some option that you forgot was available. In fact, reading the manual has to be one of the easiest — and most overlooked — ways to get better performance out of your camera.

Chapter 11

Ten Great Uses for Digital Images

*W*hen I introduce most people to their first digital camera, the exchange goes something like this:

Them: "What's that?"

Me: "It's a digital camera."

Them: "Oh." (Pause.) "What can you do with it?"

Me: "You can take digital pictures."

Them: (Thoughtful nod.) "Hmm." (Another pause, this time longer.) "And then what?"

It is at this point that the conversation takes one of two tracks: If my schedule is tight, I simply discuss the most popular use for digital photos — distributing them electronically via the

Internet. But if I have time to kill or have ingested an excess of caffeine in the past hour, I sit the person down and launch a full-fledged discussion of all the wonderful things you can do with digital images. Around this point in the conversation, the person subtly begins looking for the closest escape route and probably starts praying that the phone will ring or some other interruption will distract me. I can be, well, overly enthusiastic when it comes to this topic.

This chapter enables you to enjoy the long version of my "what you can do with digital photos" speech in the safety of your own home or office. Feel free to leave at any time — I'll be here with more ideas when you come back. But before you go, could you order some more coffee? I have a feeling that someone else might pass by soon and ask me about this funny-looking camera, and I want to be ready.

Design a More Exciting Web Site

Perhaps the most popular use for digital images is to spice up World Wide Web sites. You can include pictures of your company's product, headquarters, or staff on your Web site to help potential customers get a better idea of who you are and what you're selling.

Don't have a business to promote? That doesn't mean you can't experience the fun of participating in the Web community. Create a personal Web page for yourself or your family. Many Internet service providers make a limited amount of free space available for those who want to publish personal Web pages. And with today's Web-page creation software, the process of designing, creating, and maintaining a Web page isn't all that difficult.

E-Mail Pictures to Friends and Family

By attaching a photo to an e-mail message, you can quickly share pictures with friends, family, and colleagues around the world. No more waiting for the film lab to develop and print your pictures. No more hunting for the right size envelope to mail those pictures, and no more waiting in line at the post office to find out how many stamps you need to slap on that envelope. Just snap the picture, download it to your computer, and click the Send button in your e-mail program.

Whether you want to send a favourite aunt a picture of your new baby or send a client an image of your latest product design, the ability to communicate visual information quickly is one of the best reasons to own a digital camera.

Create Online Photo Albums

If you regularly have batches of pictures that you want to share, check out online photo-sharing sites. You can create personal digital photo albums and then invite other people to visit the site and view your pictures. Most photo-sharing sites offer printing services so that your friends and family can order copies of pictures in your albums.

Creating and maintaining an online album is easy, thanks to the user-friendly tools available today. Best of all, posting and sharing albums is usually free. You pay only for prints that you order.

To get started, check out the Black's Online PhotoCentre at `www.blackphoto.com`.

Don't rely on a photo-sharing site to store important, irreplaceable photos. If the site experiences problems, your photos could be lost. Always keep copies of your pictures on your own computer or removable storage media.

Add Impact to Sales Materials

Using a desktop publishing program such as Adobe PageMaker or Microsoft Publisher, you can easily add your digital photos to brochures, fliers, newsletters, and other marketing materials. You can also use your images in multimedia presentations created in Microsoft PowerPoint or Corel Presentations.

For best results, size your pictures to the desired dimensions and resolution in your photo software before you place them into your presentation or publishing program.

Put Your Mug on a Mug

If you own one of the new colour printers designed expressly for printing digital images, the printer may come with accessories that enable you to put your images on mugs, T-shirts, and other objects. If your software doesn't, online photo sites such as the Black's Online PhotoCentre (www.blackphoto.com) can do the job for you. The Black's Web site also provides tools that make it a snap to prepare your pictures for use in this fashion.

Call me sentimental, but I can envision these mugs being around for generations (assuming nobody breaks one, that is) to serve as a reminder of how we twentieth-century Kings once looked. Hey, 100 years ago, nobody thought that old tintype photographs would be considered heirlooms, right? So who's to say that my photographic mugs won't be treasured tomorrow? In the meantime, the family members who have laid claim to the mugs I created seem to be treasuring them today.

Print Photo Calendars and Cards

Many photo-editing programs include templates that enable you to create customized calendars featuring your images. The only decision you need to make is which picture to put on December's page and which one to use on July's. You can also find templates for designing personalized greeting cards and stationery.

If your photo editor doesn't include such templates, check the software that came with your printer. Many printers now ship with tools for creating calendars and similar projects.

When you want more than a handful of copies of your creation, you may want to have the piece professionally reproduced instead of printing each copy one by one on your own printer. You can take the job to a quick-copy shop or to a commercial service bureau or printer. Most online photo-sharing sites also offer this service.

Don't forget that the paper you use plays a large role in how professional the finished product appears. If you're printing the piece yourself, invest in some high-quality paper or special greeting-card stock, available as an accessory for many colour printers. If you're having your piece professionally printed, ask your printer for advice on which paper stock will generate the results you want.

Include Visual Information in Databases

You can add digital images to company databases and spreadsheets in order to provide employees with visual as well as text information. For example, if you work in human resources, you can insert employee pictures into your employee database. Or if you're a small-business owner and maintain a product inventory in a spreadsheet program, you can insert pictures of individual products to help you remember which items go with which order numbers. Figure 1-3 in Chapter 1 shows an example of a spreadsheet that I created in Microsoft Excel to track the inventory in my antiques shop.

Merging text and pictures in this fashion isn't just for business purposes, though. You can take the same approach to create a household inventory for your personal insurance records, for example.

Put a Name with the Face

You can put digital pictures on business cards, employee badges, and nametags for guests at a conference or other large gathering. I love getting business cards that include the person's face, for example, because I'm one of those people who never forgets a face but almost always has trouble remembering the name.

Several companies now offer special, adhesive-backed sticker paper for inkjet printers. This paper is perfect for creating badges or nametags. After printing the image, you simply stick it onto your preprinted badge or nametag.

Exchange a Picture for a Thousand Words

Don't forget the power of a photograph to convey an idea or describe a scene. Did your roof suffer damage in last night's windstorm? Take pictures of the damage and e-mail them to your insurance agent and roofing contractor. Looking for a bookcase that will fit in with your existing office decor? Take a picture of your office to the furniture store, and ask the designer for suggestions.

Written descriptions can be easily misunderstood and also take a lot longer to produce than shooting and printing a digital image. So don't tell people what you want or need — show 'em!

Hang a Masterpiece on Your Wall

Many ideas discussed in this chapter capitalize on the special capabilities that going digital offers you — the ability to display images on-screen, incorporate them into publishing projects, and so on. But you can also take a more traditional approach and simply print and frame your favourite images.

For the best-looking pictures, print your image on a dye-sub printer or photo inkjet using top-grade photo paper. If you don't own such a printer, you can take the image file to a commercial printer or photo-finishing lab. And keep in mind that prints from dye-sub and inkjet printers do fade when exposed to sunlight, so for those really important pictures, you may want to invest in a frame that has UV-protective glass. Also, hang your picture in a spot where it won't get pummelled with strong light on a regular basis, and keep a copy of the original image file so that you can reprint the image if it fades too badly.

Index